Kathleen

This is your time.

I see a Complete
Circle all in gold
all around you, This
is the light of your
higher power.

Love & Light
Carol Lovejoy

About the Author

Metaphysician. Psychic counselor. Lecturer. Many titles describe Carol Lovejoy and the work she does. Carol is a natural born psychic, and although she has several different titles, her ideas are simple and basic, an assurance of easy understanding by her many clients. Carol has experienced the psychic realm since early childhood, with experiences consisting of: spirit guides, predicting the future, feeling the vibrations of earth and people, extra terrestrials, auras, out of body, and the spiritual dimension.

Her complete healing of cancer at the age of 23 connected her to a more thorough study of healing where she studied under Dr. Robert Scott in the four year practitioners course with the Science of Mind Church. While there, she helped to coordinate the Science of Mind Church Institute Seminars where she had the honor of working with Buckminister Fuller, Olga Worrall, Dr. Irving Oyle, Dr. Norman Shealy, Dr. Elizabeth Kubler-Ross and many more outstanding people.

Her long list of credentials also includes the opportunity of having her own radio talk show at KNRY in Monterey, CA, called Mystical Adventures, Superintendent of Sunday Schools at the Science of Mind Church, and a member on the Board of Directors for the Unity Church of Modesto.

Carol's outstanding psychic abilities incorporated through her psychic counseling have helped people for over 20 years. She also has the ability to provide psychic readings over the telephone for people throughout the United States and Europe. She offers many forms of classwork, weekend retreats and Mystical tours throughout the world.

Carol's main goal in teaching is to show people how to take charge of their lives so that they will experience the maximum of love, peace, and harmony in all areas of life by seeing the past, present, and helping to create the future. This is the first book of a series of books about Carol Lovejoy's life.

For more information about private consultations, lectures, and workshops, contact:

P.O. Box 577049, Modesto, CA 95357, (209) 576-7439

"At the time I met CAROL LOVEJOY, I was reaching out for a more meaningful and abundant spiritual experience. Through Carol's counseling and workshops, not only am I gaining insights about myself, but I am also being taught techniques and disciplines that are resulting in a spiritual experience that is growing, rewarding, and downright exciting."

— BILL THOMPSON

"In the past four months my life has been dramatically affected by CAROL. My whole way of thinking has been transformed, as she has helped me to become positive and more confident."

— LESLIE REVIS

"CAROL LOVEJOY has the ability to contact people and determine currents that govern their lives. As a reading psychic, not only can she reach a specific person, but also others who may be closely associated with him or her, and thus define a functional group. Her contribution does not stop with a mere description of what she sees, because as a skilled psychotherapist, she can thus integrate emotional factors to formulate possible outcomes or courses of action. I have never met anyone who can do what she does; a powerful advisor, guide and friend."

— PAUL T. CONDIT, M.D., Ph.D.

Living in Two Worlds

By
CAROL LOVEJOY

Editor
SANDY OAKES

Cover Illustration
KATY HARDEAY

Living in Two Worlds

Copyright © 1992 by Carol Lovejoy.

Published by
GOLDEN GLOBE PUBLISHING

Typography
TEMPEL TYPOGRAPHICS

Printing
GRIFFIN PRINTING & LITHOGRAPH CO. INC.

Library of Congress Cataloging-in-Publication Data
LC 92-081954

Lovejoy, Carol.
Living in Two Worlds / Carol Lovejoy
p. cm.

ISBN 0-9633137-6-2

This book is dedicated to my two daughters,
Tammy and Stacy, whose love,
support, and understanding
helped make my journey possible.

With a special appreciation to
Sandy Oakes, my editor,
whose thoughtfulness and dedication
helped bring this book into publication.

Many thanks to Tammy for all the work of
helping to organize the people and paperwork
to get this book out to the world.

I give
Love and Light to John and Raa
for the teachers and
protectors they are.

This is a true story.

*Some of the names and places in this book
have been changed to protect
the privacy of those involved.*

Contents

CHAPTER ONE

Life

The smell of charred and blackened bodies, mixed with the acrid smell of human blood, invaded the cold night air. The stench overwhelmed me, threatening to overturn my already weakened, nauseated stomach.

The black smoke hung heavy in the sky, making each breath its own battle. As I looked up into the sky to find a clean breath of air, a brilliant flash erupted momentarily lighting the gray smoke up in a silver burst. Cannons roared in reply, shaking the ground beneath my feet, unsteadying my already unsteady body. I wanted so badly to move, run, hide! But my body refused to move, it developed a mind of its own, and that mind was frozen in fear.

I closed my eyes in pain. I didn't have to look to know what was out there. Bodies, pieces of bodies, human flesh, littered the snow, marking the exact points of a misfortunate shelling's impact.

Once again I heard the cannons and felt, rather than saw, the deadly flash of light. I opened my eyes quickly to search out a safe hiding place in the briefly illuminated battle field. All I saw was the hundreds of fallen German soliders, their bodies and faces a matching mixture of pain and fear, each lying in his own frozen pool of blood, like an embryonic fluid surrounding a baby. Except this was the fluid of death,

1

not the fluid of life. I turned away quickly, not wishing to make eye contact with their blank, staring, dead eyes.

My body ached from the bitter cold. I weakly tried to warm my hands with my breath, a vain attempt to turn them back to skin color, for I didn't recognize the purple and red frostbitten extremities that were once my hands. I tried to move my feet, but a sharp stabbing of pain shot up my legs. Which was worse: being in pain from frozen limbs, or being frozen with fear? I didn't know the answer, nor did I wish to discover it. Slowly, but surely, I felt death wrap around me like a warm, beckoning blanket, promising to thaw my frozen limbs and fear.

The shelling stopped abruptly and a loud silence replaced it. The silence hung in the air as if life itself had stopped. Then the thundering silence became my enemy. I knew my enemy was closing in on me, stealthily waiting to strike, a snake coiled and waiting, venom hot in its deadly bite.

This would make even the strongest man mad, I thought frantically, knowing death's hand was reaching out of that smoking sky.

A twig snapped behind me, signaling the silence was over. I turned quickly, ignoring the pain shooting up my legs. I pointed my gun toward the noise, the weapon ice cold and wet stuck to my frostbitten skin, pulling flesh away from muscle and bone. I felt my heart pounding in my throat, threatening to explode inside my neck with its fierce beating. Once again I became frozen as fear grabbed its icy hand around me.

"No closer, I'll kill you!" I heard myself scream in a voice unrecognizable to me. I was a voice of frenzy, a voice crazed with the desire to live and a voice violently afraid of inevitable death. "I'll kill you!"

"Kill me, honey?" I heard a woman's voice asking warmly, making me sit bolt upright in my bed, awakening me from the clutches of my troubled sleep.

I blinked my eyes open, ready for enemy soldiers to rush

at me from every angle, but instead saw the figure of my mother sitting at the foot of my bed. Her eyes filled with love and understanding. On the table near her sat a candle, whose every flicker of light caressed her face, softening her normal features which always seemed to be lined with worry and overwork.

"Oh, Mama, they're going to kill me," I cried, flying into her arms and snuggling deep into her lap, welcoming her warm embrace.

"No one is going to kill you, honey. We all love you here, you know that," she murmured gently, kissing me on the top of my head, and smoothing my damp and tousled hair.

"But the war, Mama!" I pleaded. "The American soldiers have me surrounded, and are going to kill me because I'm a Nazi!"

"Shh!" she whispered sternly, rocking me in her arms. "We'll have no talk of Nazis or of wars, Carol. You're not a Nazi, and there isn't a war."

"But there is, Mama!" I stated indignantly, as I brushed back the tears now running freely down my cheeks, then wiped my nose on my nightgown sleeve.

"Carol, do you know what a Nazi is?" my mother asked, as she reached into the pocket of her robe for a handkerchief.

"No," I whispered, pouting as I blew my nose into the handkerchief my mother held out in front of me.

"Then that settles it, Carol," my mother replied, matter-of-factly in her don't-ask-me-anything-else tone, and placed the handkerchief back into her pocket. She stood and pulled back the covers on the bed, leaving me sitting on the bed alone.

"It's time to go back to bed, Carol," she said.

"But Mama," I whimpered, as I crawled on all fours from the foot of the bed to where my pillow rested quietly, waiting my return.

"But nothing, young lady," my mother scolded as she pulled the bed covers up under my chin and tucked me into bed. "Nazi's were bad people, Carol, and I don't want to hear about them ever again. Do you understand?"

I nodded my head automatically in reply, showing her I understood (although I knew I really didn't) and clutched the covers up to my mouth.

"That's a good girl," Mama said approvingly, and kissed me on the forehead. She wished me sweet dreams and left my room, taking with her the light of the candle.

For a few moments I could see her shadow against my wall as she walked down the hallway, and I clung to her protective image. Her darkly silhouetted form danced against the warm light of the flickering candle, its light dispelled the lurking shadows of my room. Then suddenly her shadow was gone, and so was the light, and with the diminishing light came back my fear. Drapes suddenly became ominous things, as they fluttered in the breeze of partially opened windows. They were unnatural specters, enemy soldiers who hid in inky darkness, stealthily waiting for me. Clothes tossed thoughtlessly on the floor became goblins of immeasurable heights. In my imagination I could hear the scraping of their long, taloned claws against the hardwood floor as they crept closer, grunting and drooling with the effort of pulling their fat, black scaly bellies behind them. They became hideous, faceless apparitions that at any moment would be within range to pounce upon their helpless victim, shaking with fear on the bed. I grabbed the blankets over my head before they could advance any further, feeling completely safe in my protective cocoon. I had thwarted any sneak attacks from soldiers or goblin armies, and I smiled at my ingenuity as I pulled the covers closer around me. I didn't have much time to congratulate myself since within minutes I fell fast asleep.

I awoke as the first streaks of the dawning sun entered my window. I breathed in deeply the fragrance of fresh-mown hay and autumn. I looked around my room for any signs of soldiers or goblins, and found that they had gone. Perhaps, I mused, they had decided to march off to frighten some other little boy or girl where darkness still prevailed. Then I giggled to myself for beating them at their own game.

Proud of my accomplishment, I jumped out of bed with the excitement of a normal child who felt she had been given a second chance at life. I dressed hurriedly in a cotton dress, pulled on a pair of worn brown leather shoes, made my bed as best I could, and bounded out into the kitchen where I knew my mother would greet me. The smell of homemade biscuits, oatmeal and coffee filled the air, and my stomach growled in spite of itself with happy anticipation.

My mother looked beautiful as she worked over the old white stove. She lightly hummed a gospel tune while she busily stirred oatmeal one minute, then checked the coffee next. She was so involved with her cooking that she hadn't noticed my entry. I seized upon the opportunity and reached over to the kitchen table where hot, fat flaky biscuits were piled high on a polished tin platter, steaming the air. Adeptly, I grabbed one and tucked it into my dress pocket before my mother could notice. The warmth radiated through the thin fabric of my dress, and felt good against my skin. The action caught my mother's eye, and she turned toward me and smiled.

"Well, my little soldier is the first one up," she chided, pointing a wooden spoon in my direction, pieces of oatmeal still sticking in its bowl. "War is a hard business, I suppose," she joked, smiling as she put the spoon down on top of the stove. I knew she wasn't making fun of me, just pretended to be, so I smiled back.

"Well, Carol, I'm glad you got out with your skin," she continued, with a gleam of understanding in her eyes, and squatted down with her arms extended.

I flew into her arms and hugged her tightly forgetting my biscuit, crushing it with my embrace.

"I love you, Mama," I said, meaning every word, enjoying the fresh clean soap scent of her skin and the safe warmth of her body.

She kissed my forehead lightly and held me tighter. "I love you, too, Carol. Always know that," she replied calmly, then released me and stood up to stir the oatmeal once again.

After breakfast my father and brothers were dismissed to do various chores, and I helped with the dishes; drying the chipped plates and stained cups until they reflected objects like tiny mirrors. I folded my white linen dishtowel neatly and gave it to my mother, anticipating her next reply.

"Well, Carol, I don't have anything else for you to do right now, but stay close outside in case I think of something," my mother clucked, drying her hands on her calico apron.

"Yes, Mama," I replied, running out the door, knowing full well that if I didn't hurry my mother would "think of something" momentarily.

The warm autumn sun greeted me as I ran down the front porch steps. The sound of birds filled the air and blended beautifully with the soft lowing of the cows in the distance. It was a wonderful day and I rejoiced at being alive, being a part of this magical moment.

I skipped out toward the road, feeling the sun warm my back, and noticed my shadow stretched out and distorted in front of me. I stopped my skipping. It stopped too. I raised my arms and flapped like a wild bird. The shadow flapped as well. I was intrigued by the mirror-like movement of my inky shadow reflection, and noticed the colors radiating from the shadow figure. Green and yellow encircled my shadow head, creating a brilliant contrast to the blackness. Fascinated, I watched the colors change and move about my shadow. All of a sudden, another shadow appeared next to mine. It had the broad shape of a man, a man that somehow I felt I knew, or as if it were important that I knew.

No longer satisfied with just seeing his shadow, I turned toward its creator. He was dressed like everyone I knew, a farmer of some type, as his faded overalls and red plaid flannel shirt indicated. His hair was a golden blond which curled youthfully around his head.

My attention was swayed by a huge cat beside him. I had never seen a cat so large, and it had the most beautiful coat of orange and black stripes. I was instantly at ease with this pair. They were figures I had seen before, I just couldn't quite remember where. Their presence did not frighten me one bit, although I struggled with their placement in my memory.

"Hello, Carol, my name is John," the man said with a twinkle in his clear blue eyes. He pointed to the large cat beside him. "And this is Raa."

I smiled a hello and began to stroke the fur of the animal, which felt as soft as it looked. A low purr rumbled from the cat's throat in a greeting as he began to rub his head against my shoulder. The force of the large animal almost knocked me over, and I giggled at the prospect.

"Raa and I are happy to see you, Carol. It's been a while," he said simply, with a familiar grin.

I laughed out loud. Not at what he had said but from the tickle of Raa's sandpaper tongue on my face. I had a peculiar feeling of oneness with these two characters, as though I was finally at home. I felt truly happy, and without reason I laughed again.

"Now how am I supposed to teach you anything if you keep giggling all day?" John asked sternly, but that twinkle in his eyes betrayed his stern tone.

I laughed again, against my will, as my attention was diverted from John by Raa who pushed affectionately against me, nudging me into an unlady-like heap on the dirt road.

"Carol!" John barked suddenly, instantly commanding my attention from my sitting-down position on the road. Then more gently he added, "I noticed you were studying the colors in your shadow."

I nodded my head in reply as he helped me up to a standing position. I forgot to even dust off the back of my clothes, so intrigued I was about the colors and how they got into my shadow. I had a million questions, like what did they mean?

John continued the game that I had earlier started with my shadow, and we both moved and watched the bright colors in our shadows.

"Look at the green dancing around your head," John remarked in excitement. "What do you think that would say about someone?"

I stopped my play to think about that question, but try as I might, I couldn't find a sufficient answer. John noticed my confused look and prompted me gently.

"Well, think about what's green," he said.

Thinking for a moment and searching around me, I came out with, "Leaves, grass, things that grow . . ."

"How right you are!" John exclaimed. "Growth, you are experiencing growth, that's what the green color in your shadow tells you. You see, these colors tell you who you are. Color is energy and this color in your shadow is your vibration, telling you who you are inside."

Excited by his information, I looked back into my shadow to see if there were other colors dancing around it. Sure enough, I saw a radiant orange moving about my head, shimmering in a prism-like brilliance. "Look!" I exclaimed, jumping up and down with excitement. "Look at the orange. What does it mean, John?"

John began to laugh at my uncontrollable excitement.

"Look at how happy and alive with excitement you are. The orange is telling you that you're alive with energy and you excited about your experience."

In the faint distance I heard my name being called. My mother's voice rang out sweet and clear in the stillness of the afternoon. I followed the voice with my eyes and saw her standing on the front steps, wiping her hands on her apron in an all-to-well motherly gesture.

I turned back to John and Raa, a reluctance to leave them was evident in my features. I couldn't leave now, not when I was beginning to learn so much.

John took my small hand into his large one. He looked right into my eyes and told me we would play again tomorrow. There was no doubt he was telling the truth, I could see his sincerity clearly in his blue eyes.

I gave Raa a pat on the head before I turned and ran off toward the house. Right before entering, I glanced back in a parting gesture, but my two friends were out of sight.

The screen door banged with finality leaving me with the vivid memory of the day's events and my two new friends I made.

That night I found myself once again in Germany. My house was splendid, and I glowed with pride as I walked up to our circular driveway. Huge towering stone spires pierced into the sky on either side of the building, framing the central portion of the house which contained thirty-two rooms in all. The frosted windows of each room were lit, the outside light soon swallowed by the continuous cascade of tiny snowflakes fluttering quietly to the ground. The lawn and grounds were completely blanketed in the glistening snow, making the grounds look like an ice castle out of some child's fairytale. The snow crunched noisily as I walked up the front steps to my door. A wreath of holly and pine graced its polished wood frame. I turned the burnished bronze knob with my black leather-gloved hand and opened the door. Warmth, the sweet smell of cooking food and cheery "hello's" greeted me as I entered the house.

"God bless, Master Carl, and a Merry Christmas to you!" Ziegfried, our fat butler, quipped as he bustled about the hallway, securing holiday garlands of holly and mistletoe at the bottom of our grand stairway.

The house was alive with merriment. I smiled as I watched the hurried pace of our servants hustling about the rooms, taking care of last minute decorating and craftily positioning tasty delicacies on sprawling tables for easy perusal and nibbling by the guests. I walked through the hallway into the main room, almost bumping into a blushing maid-servant juggling two silver trays laden with little pink and white iced cakes. I sought out the warmth of the cheery fire in the study, took off my gloves, and extended my hands near the flaming log which crackled happily in the hearth.

Ziegfried approached with a silver tray of liquor to warm me and I gratefully accepted a glass. I drank it down with one gulp, placed it back on the tray and reached for another.

"Your father is asking to see you, Carl," Ziegfried said, smiling as he watched my actions.

As he spoke, the house disappeared. No longer did I hold a glass of liquor, but a bayonet. The fire I stood against was no longer contained in a hearth, but lay scattered across a smokey battlefield. Deafening explosions rang in my ears, planes buzzed loudly across the sky. I began to run, and the sound of bullets whizzed near my head. I had to get across the field. I had to get across, my feet feeling like heavy lead as I ran. My destination was so close, so close. I was almost there, almost . . . almost. A bright explosion of red and orange blasted in front of me and I shrieked with fear.

The panic I felt jarred me awake, and I gasped for air. It was morning. I was safely back in my little farm room. I buried my face in my shaking hands, trying to dislodge the horrible pictures still pouring through my mind. My heart thumped rapidly against my chest, as if any minute it would break out and jump away. I took a deep breath, trying to settle my nerves, and remind myself it was just a dream. There was a damp chill in the air. I looked outside through my window, but sheets of water obscured my view. The glass began to rattle with every new gust, sending the outside shutter banging to and fro. A jagged flash of lightning ripped open the gloomy darkness of the sky and I jumped at the blast of thunder, sounding much too similar to the explosions in my nightmare.

I dressed and went to breakfast, picking over my

untouched food. Disappointment and restless sleep curbed my normal appetite, as I knew with certainty that the rain would end any hope I had of meeting John and Raa. My mother always kept us in on Saturday, since it was our normal holy day. Usually, a time for prayers and Bible reading, but now with the onslaught of such nasty weather it would be all but impossible to sneak away unnoticed.

We finished with our private service at noon, therefore I was free to do what I wanted, so I immediately sought out the haven of the bedroom and began to play.

"Hello, Carol," a familiar voice boomed in unison with a happy purr.

I straightened my head immediately at the sound, and who was there to catch my bewildered gaze, but John and Raa, who both seemed to exude a pale gold aura of light which contrasted greatly with the semi-darkness of my room. John was sitting nonchalantly at the foot of my bed, while Raa lay stretched across its length. Both seemed happy to see me. I ran to John, sat securely on his lap, and hugged him firmly in greeting.

"Thought we'd forget you today, did you?" he smiled, a twinkle in his clear blue eyes. With a wink to Raa he picked me up and sat me next to him on the bed.

"How did you get here?" I inquired, now over my recent surprise and excitement.

"Everything is possible when you believe enough," he stated with a dramatic wave of his hands.

"But that doesn't explain . . ." I started, but was interrupted by one of my brothers who suddenly entered my room.

"Quit talkin' to yourself, Carol," he sneered.

"I'm not talking to myself. Can't you see John and Raa are here? Are you blind or something?" I answered back, pointing to my two friends.

"I don't see nothin'!" Ricky yelled back adamantly.

"You don't?" I asked him, my voice trailing off, as I looked

looked back at John, who just shrugged and looked away from me.

By the time I had turned around to confront my brother, he had already left. Only boyish laughter, laced with the chant, "Carol's talking to herself," could be heard down the hall. I looked at John in astonishment. "Why can't he see you?" I asked quietly, a little bit afraid.

"Because he doesn't want to," John replied easily. "You only open yourself up to things that you believe to be true, and since we are not a part of his life, he doesn't accept us as real. I am sure he could see us if he wanted to. He could see anything that he believes to be real to him. Remember that energy makes up everything, therefore thoughts are energy. So if you didn't believe this house, which is made up of energy existed, it wouldn't. The same with Raa and I, we would exist someplace else in our own reality or someone else's.

"You see, energy is always energy. You can't destroy it, only rearrange it, either on this earth dimension or on a spiritual level. Energy never dies, only changes its form. It's always up to you to choose which time, or place, or people you want to surround yourself with, and you can tap into the present, past and future at will. You are a being without limitations or boundaries. Therefore you have the ability to transcend any time, and to journey through any and all dimensions of the universe. This ability begins with the understanding of energy and identifying the soul. You already know a little about energy, so today it's time we begin to learn about the soul," John said, and clasped his hands together in his lap.

"But Ricky can't see you," I repeated, still unsure of John's explanation.

"Probably no one but you can see us, Carol," John stated. "Does that bother you?"

"N-No," I stammered, still somewhat shaken by this strange discovery.

"We are real, as real as anything you see around you. We could manifest ourselves and make it so everyone could see us, but it would disrupt people unnecessarily, and the extra energy we would use to complete the task would drain from the things around us, as we would have to take some energy from surrounding people and things. The whole process would be rather tiring and utterly bothersome, so I'd rather not have to do it to make a point. You can see us right now and that's all that really matters, isn't it?"

I nodded my head in agreement as John placed his arm around my shoulders. His arm was warm and the weight of it was reassuring. If he were a figment of my imagination, then so was the bed I sat on and the house I lived in. My understanding of things grew less and less secure, but I didn't care because I had friends who loved me. They made me feel safe, and put my mind and body at ease.

We sat that way for a few minutes as I listened to the soft sound of the rain pounding on our roof. I always liked the quiet melody of the rain, its resonance a peaceful song, whose lyrics I imagined were carried and whispered by beautiful mermaids far out to sea.

"Come along, Carol, we have things to do," John said as he stood.

I followed him over to the dresser with Raa tagging silently behind.

"Here is where we learn how to see the soul," John said triumphantly, his face beaming with anticipation.

"Here?" I inquired, looking around the room, wondering why he had chosen this particular place.

"This seems to be the only mirror in your home," he replied, his hand pointing to the old mirror above the dresser.

"A mirror?" I echoed in bewilderment.

"It's the simplest way to see your soul, Carol," John explained, as he hoisted me up closer to the mirror in such a way that my face rested only inches away from my reflection.

"Since the body and your energy is only a reflection of the soul, we need to look past the physical and into yourself. The reflection you see of yourself in the mirror is you, but only a facsimile of your true self sitting at the dresser. It's the same with the soul, your body is like the reflection; it's you, but not the true being of you. It is an image created by the soul that is allowed to manifest on this earth level. Your true being, then, is not what you see but only a projection of a higher, spiritual self. Therefore, we must travel on a bridge, so to speak, from one view you have of self to another. The bridge we walk across lies through the eyes.

"Now you can see a reflection of your reflection in your eyes. A miniature self contained in your pupil. Now we have self looking at self, looking at self. Now relax, and go beyond your miniature self you view in your eyes. Go beyond the physical barrier and walk across the bridge to soul."

Within seconds I found myself viewing a golden luminous light of rotating and spinning energy, and as it spun it glittered like a perfectly cut diamond. Its center was a brilliant whirling mass of golden light, a spinning luminous egg of energy. Tiny particles of colored light, pastel pinks, greens and blues, would seemingly emerge from this center and orbit it with amazing speed, then disappear only to have another emerge in its place. I had never seen or experienced anything so perfectly beautiful, and I sat hypnotized as I stared at my soul energy through my eyes in the mirror. It continued to sparkle and pulsate, and I began to be drawn deeper into its center, becoming a part of this wondrous sight. As I ventured deeper into the experience, I no longer saw or felt my body, only the ecstasy of the brilliant energy. Music sweeter than I had ever heard or could have imagined filled my senses as I began to blend with the core of my being. As I reached center, I felt love inside and out, flowing through every part of my being.

Every question I had ever asked was answered in that moment. Every understanding of the universe, from the dawn of creation was mine. I felt a joining with hundreds upon thousands of souls, connecting with them all. An excitement of wonder and love began to grow through my being as I felt my soul vibrating faster and faster with each new insight. I became caught up in the spinning energy until I felt as if I would burst from its intensity. Suddenly it became a dance to which I did not know the steps, could not keep the pace, and I retreated from it. In doing so, I lost the image in my mind and found myself sitting in front of the old dresser once again.

I instantly began to concentrate once again on my eye in the mirror, but was interrupted by John.

"That's enough soul watching for today, Carol," he chided, a smile of approval belying his gruff manner. "Now tell me what you saw."

"A beautiful sparkling diamond," I replied eagerly.

"Did you see or feel anything else?" he asked.

"I saw hundreds of colored lights circling around the diamond, almost like they were planets in the solar system circling our sun. And, oh, I felt such love, John, I thought I could bask in the love forever. I heard music, beautiful music that must have been sung by a hundred angels. I was happy there, until everything began to go faster and faster, and I could not concentrate on who or what I was. I felt as if I was taking on too much at once. I just kinda lost the picture after that," I ended, still sitting, looking up at John.

"The colors you saw are the feelings and thought patterns that we have carried with us and experienced from lifetime to lifetime. We have all gone through so much that we can only carry so many memories of past lifetimes with us in our present state of reality, but our soul keeps a constant record of each lifetime. It stores every thought, every emotion and every feeling we have ever experienced throughout our entire existence. Everything we have ever been or will be is contained in the soul, the center of which is perfect love and understanding. The soul only knows love, it cannot hate."

He paused for a moment to see if I had grasped his meaning, and when he saw that I understood, he once again continued. "Law is the order of the universe. Everyone has different work to do. This work is Law in motion. We are on earth voluntarily, striving and hoping that we can learn how to love ourselves, the universe and its creatures. You probably remember that in the Bible prophets wrote, '. . . as you sow, so shall you reap.' This is the perfect concept of Law or karma. If you hurt someone in a past, present, or future lifetime, you are allowing the effects of negative Law or karma to go into play. The same is true if you help someone and feel love, this is positive karma. The soul will record this incident, and place you in a similar situation where you can repay this debt, and experience the same love or pain you consciously willed on another. The soul is not 'bad' in doing this, but simply putting you in a position where you can experience different situations in order to facilitate your fastest spiritual growth."

"I didn't feel any of that," I said, unhappy I had missed part of my lesson.

"You will know when the moment presents itself. Next time instead of focusing on the center of the soul, look into the colors orbiting around it. You will be able to see and understand what I'm talking about. You can develop an ability to see the colors reflected around each person's outer body just like when you saw the colors surrounding your shadow the other day. By doing this, you will have an idea what each person is thinking and feeling, or know some of the karma they are carrying with them in this life."

"How do I do that?" I started, excited with the prospect of reading people's thoughts and feelings.

"Look back into the mirror, Carol."

*The seen and the unseen
are they not one?*

Expand your sight

Illumination, Light

*Look within soul
into the mirror of life.*

See the unseen

Expand your sight

Illumination, Colors, Light

CHAPTER TWO

Soul

"Now concentrate on looking at your forehead. Try to blur your normal vision and look through the world with soft eyes. Just squint a little. Now as you look at your forehead, start expanding your vision out around to your head and shoulder area. Now, clear your mind and focus on the area around your head. Just relax into the experience and tell me what you see."

I blurred my vision and glanced into the mirror, squinting like my older brother Mark does when he forgets to put on his glasses. I sat that way for just a little while, when quite suddenly a faint glow surrounded my head and shoulders. Where only nothingness once existed, a halo of intense beauty now glittered.

"What do you see, Carol?" John asked, bending his head next to mine. I could see a golden light glowing inches above my head.

"A halo!" I exclaimed excitedly. "Like the angels!"

"Every living thing carries this halo with them, Carol. It's not just confined to celestial entities, or angels, as you call them. You may have seen paintings of people who are depicted with one of these halos around them. This rim of light you see is like a shell of energy around you. Picture an egg shell and how it holds the egg together. The first thing

we see when we start to look at energy is this golden glow.
It's around trees and plant life, as well as animal life.

"The color gold means infinite wisdom. It has the power
to filter out negative energy and helps to keep you healthy."

All through John's dissertation I listened to what he was
saying, but continued to look at myself in the mirror. And
while he was talking, I noticed my halo was not stationary
like those in the paintings, but instead continued to move.
One moment the light would manifest near my temple, only
to disappear then reappear over my head. Soon that area of
bright energy would reshape again, until it entirely covered
my shoulder area, then just as quickly shrank in size back to
my temple where it originated. I was fascinated by the
shifting light, and moved my head back and forth in front of
the mirror, smiling as the energy trailed behind me. I giggled
as it caught up with my movements, and watched it settle
around my head where once again it began to dance and
reshape its form.

"Now keep focusing on the aura of light around you and
tell me what you see," John coaxed.

I didn't need any encouragement from him, since I knew
at this point I would have a hard time concentrating on
anything else. I was held captive in the shimmering flux of
light.

Gradually, I could see faint colors beginning to bleed
through the fabric of my aura, displacing the golden light.
First a dark purple, then a clear green, and finally a faint sky
blue appeared and danced above my head. I opened my
mouth to say something to John, then a flash of yellow burst
amid the colors. It surprised me so much with its intensity
that instead of voicing my objections, I simply gaped open-
mouthed at myself in the mirror.

"Pretty, isn't it?" John queried, winking at the reflection
of myself in the mirror.

"Yes, it is!" I agreed, regaining my ability to speak.

"Now look at my aura, Carol," John quipped, a gentle

smile gracing his features.

And as I looked at him, I became surprised I hadn't seen any colors around him before. Magnificent iridescent blues and indigo purples, flecked with flashes of gold and silver light, radiated a foot or so around him. It looked as if he carried the stars and twilight sky upon his shoulders. He appeared so beautiful to me that a small gasp escaped my lips in wonder.

"Do you like it?" John inquired, flashing a haughty smile as he struck a model's pose.

I almost thought he was asking my opinion in the purchase of a new hat or coat, not his aura. The comment caught me off guard and I laughed at his comical antics.

"What's so funny?" John grumbled, feigning hurt feelings with a childish pout.

"You are," I answered with a high giggle.

"Good!" he said exuberantly, bending down on one knee to face me. "Laughter is good for the soul. It rids the mind and body of tension, balancing our physical and emotional body. It helps us get rid of the old garbage, so to speak, such as anger, pain and loneliness.

"Carol, look at your colors now while you are still laughing."

I looked around me quickly and saw a brilliant violet hue completely surrounding me.

"Violet is the color of cleansing," John began to explain to me while I was still mesmerized by the beautiful color. "It's like giving your energy field a shower. You wash off all the old negative feelings that you have been carrying around with you."

The deep blue was coming back and concentrating around my shoulders.

"I see you like that blue surrounding you," John commented, smiling at my obvious pleasure. "That blue is the color of spiritual calm and confidence. Look inside the blue and tell me what you see." John kept his focus strictly on me.

I looked deeper into the beautiful blue and I saw a cross that seemed to be attached to my back between my shoulder blades. "What does the cross mean?" I asked him, never taking my eyes off it.

"The cross is a symbol of karma or universal law. For you, Carol, it means that you have come into this life to work in the spiritual, and it shows in your aura," John said.

"John—" I started to ask him another question when my mother's voice pierced our concentration.

"Carol! Supper's ready," she called again from the kitchen. I yelled a reply and stood up to leave for supper.

"Carol," John paused me for a moment. "I have an idea. Why don't we practice our new lesson by studying your family's colors?"

I thought it was a great idea and nodded my head enthusiastically.

"Go to dinner and Raa and I will be with you and help you to see everyone's energy fields," John whispered inside my head. By the time he was finished, both he and Raa had begun to vaporize before my eyes.

Bodies were gradually replaced by solid golden forms of energy, entirely surrounded by halos of sapphire blue. As I watched, the forms pulled completely into the center, until only two blue balls of light floated in the air, and within seconds were gone.

"Just listen," I heard John say, as the last speck of blue energy dissolved into nothingness before me, leaving me suddenly alone in the room.

"Carol," my mother called again, this time louder than before.

"Coming," I answered and, stunned by what I had witnessed, ran down the hall to the kitchen as fast as my legs could carry me. I slowed down as I came to the kitchen and paused at the hallway door sill. I was amazed by the sight that greeted me. It wasn't my family that surprised me, but the multitude of colors radiating from around their bodies.

I suddenly lived in a world of rainbows and stood gaping in awe as I viewed my family from this new perspective.

"You see, our lesson isn't over yet," I heard John clearly explaining to me.

"What?" I responded automatically out loud, as my brother Ricky passed me, walking to the kitchen table.

"I didn't say anything!' he stormed, pushing past me as he sat down at the table and grabbed a piece of cornbread, stuffing it into his mouth greedily.

"What do you mean?" I thought, figuring that speaking in thoughts would be safer than any vocalization.

"Look at him, Carol. Look at what he's carrying with him," John instructed.

I noticed his aura was a complete murky red, except for areas where it mixed with black and grey. Instinctively, I was repelled by it, and quickly diverted my eyes to the table which was heaped with plates of black-eyed peas and cornbread.

"These are the colors of anger, frustration and confusion," John explained. "Clear red, in itself, is a beautiful color. It represents basic life force energy. It gives us physical strength and stamina. But he has so much confusion and anger, he turns his physical strength into being pushy and a bully."

This explanation made sense to me. Ricky was always getting into fights and pulling pranks on people. I remembered how he hung my doll from a tree and left it there, out of my reach, for days just to be mean.

"There you are," my mother scolded, handing me a metal potato masher and instructed me to finish the job. "So, you've admired yourself in the mirror all afternoon, Carol? A funny thing to do on a Sabbath after a morning of prayers," she remarked with a coolness in her tone.

"I was looking at my soul and seeing it's beauty," I replied truthfully.

She laughed a funny laugh and started to hum one of her favorite spiritual hymns.

Over her humming, I heard John whisper in my head.

"Carol, you better keep quiet about your experience or they'll think you're nuts, and your brothers will really have something to tease you about."

I made the motion of "zipping my lips" shut. Then I turned my attention back to my mother, carefully watching her movements. I saw a strange yellow over her head, dark mustard in color, pierced with black lines, closely resembling the grooves in a worn record. All around this yellow was a deep red with some blue specks flecked in it.

John's voice spoke to me again inside my head, "That dark yellow means your mother lives in her head. She thinks about everything all the time and she's really emotional. She spends her days in a state of worry, thinking about things she can do nothing about. The black lines show a long pattern of worry. Whenever these rings or patterns are present, it shows worry has become so ingrained that it has become a habit. That explains why she's tired all the time, these types of patterns drain her energy right out of her."

I instantly felt the love I felt earlier in soul energy come up through me and flow out to her.

She shook with cold-like chills all over her body as she felt the love embrace her being. The blue specks seemed to get brighter when this happened.

"Blue is her spiritual energy," John remarked. "On her spiritual level, she accepted the love you just gave her, Carol."

Just then my mother turned her attention on me.

"That's good, honey," my mother said, taking the mashed potatoes from me, her voice seemingly much softer than before.

The door startled us as it slammed open with two of my brothers, David and Peter, running through it. They were teasing and laughing at my skinny brother, Mark, who tagged shyly behind.

Clear blues, soft pinks and brilliant greens touched with hues of watermelon red exploded around David and Peter as they scurried across the room to the sink where they washed their hands, splashing water on each other as they played.

Mark waited to wash up until they were finished drying their hands and were seated at the table. He slowly walked across the room to the basin next to where I stood and placed his wire-rimmed glasses on the drain board, squinting as he turned the knob of the faucet. Unlike Peter or David, Mark seemed encased in a grey cloud that was concentrated the heaviest around his eyes, settling in a grey fog. The only other discernible colors were a lime green and dark yellow above his head and a dirty red which wrapped tightly around his throat area, but even these colors were dimmed by the shroud of grey mist surrounding him.

"Your brothers, Peter and David, are happy individuals, Carol," John's voice said. "They wear the colors of green, blue and pink with touches of red. The red just shows they are up to some harmless mischief, just an excitement for living, nothing more. Green is the color of growth and inner balance. Peter and David are learning and growing through their play. The pink you see is love even though Mark doesn't feel it, Peter and David's joking and teasing is all done with love."

I began to walk across the room to the table, where I sat next to David. He was the closest to my own age and my best friend. I was happy with John's description of him and gave his hand a tiny squeeze in secret joy.

By this time Mark had finished washing his hands and had seated himself across from me at the table. As I turned away from the table to watch my mother complete her task, John's voice once again interrupted my thoughts.

"What do you think about Mark's aura?" he asked, drawing my attention back to the lanky boy who sat glumly across from me.

"It's not very pretty," I thought in reply.

"No, it's not," John remarked with concern. "He's covered himself with a cloud of depression. He can't cope

with the world around him, so he has created a wall of
negativity to keep everything away. The lime green shows his
envy of others and the dark yellow, his negative thinking. He
doesn't like himself much, Carol, and he is choking himself
with emotional frustration. The red wraps his throat like a
noose and cuts off his ability to communicate with people,
and the more frustrated he gets the more it tightens. He has
become a hermit type and his own worst enemy. How sad
and lonely it would be to have only yourself to talk to,
especially when that is who you despise the most. Notice the
fog around his eyes, Carol. His negativity has blinded him to
the outside world. He's created his own world of self loathing
so completely that no pair of glasses will ever help him see
himself or life in its true perspective. Be kind to him, Carol,
he needs it very much."

My heart went out to Mark and I noticed a little change
in his colors.

Once again the front door opened, and it was my father
who walked into the room. He was a tall thin man, who
always wore a gentle smile, through happiness as well as
adversity. I felt a warm glow of energy come up through me
and spin out from my heart area toward my father.

He walked over to me and rubbed my head affectionately.

Looking right into my eyes, he said, "How are you,
Kitten?"

"Come wash up, Slim, dinner's ready," Mama interrupted
our special moment.

"Yes, Jewell," my father calmly replied, walking over to
the sink and kissing my mother on the cheek before running
the water.

When everyone was seated, I began to look at my
father's aura. Even through the evening prayer, when we all
were supposed to bow our heads and concentrate on the
words, I snuck looks at him. He had yellows like the yellow
that was spread around me. John whispered that my father
liked to think and learn. That's why he reads everyday. Then

I saw this ball of pink come from him and surround everyone at the table.

"He loves his family," John remarked. "Carol, feel the love."

Then I saw a large cross above his head and this cross went up to a large dark hole hovering above his head. The cross seemed as though it was going to pull my father through the dark hole. I forced myself to look closely into the hole, hesitating, because I felt I wasn't going to like what I saw. Inside the hole was a grave with a large tombstone looming next to it. I was so frightened, I felt frozen in place, my heartbeat seemed to stop and my hands felt cold and numb. "John," I said silently to myself. "John, what is it? What is it?" I repeated it until I realized John was not going to answer my question. He wasn't even there any longer. What did this mean? I only had myself to ask the rest of the evening and I couldn't come up with any answers.

"It's time for bed, children," Mama clucked, as the clock struck seven-thirty. Dozens of protests filled the air, promptly overridden by my father, and one by one my brothers stomped down the hall to their bedrooms. I usually would have pleaded to stay up later, but the words would not come. Instead I sat mutely on the floor, ignoring my other siblings, continuing to watch my father sitting in his chair.

"Let's go, Carol," Mama urged, clapping her hands together, trying to round me up as she would her chickens.

"Wait a minute, Jewell," my father interrupted, sitting up in his old fabric chair, the arms frayed and split with use. "I want to talk to Carol."

"Alright, Slim," Mama agreed halfheartedly. "But only for a few minutes." She began to busy herself in the kitchen.

"What's the matter with my favorite girl?" he asked, his voice warm and soothing as the sunshine. "You've been quiet all evening, and you seem to stay by yourself more and more."

"I'm worried about you, your color is all off!" I cried,

running across the room and jumping into his lap.

"My color?" he smiled, tousling my hair with a big calloused hand. "Don't be silly, I feel great. Tomorrow will be a beautiful day, full of wonder and surprises. Just enjoy this world, every minute, and don't let any gloomy thoughts make you sad."

"I was, well, just worried," I whispered, playing with a button on his shirt.

"Why do you spend so much time by yourself, Kitten?" he asked.

"I don't, I'm with my friends, John and Raa," I replied truthfully, looking into his warm velvet brown eyes. "John says you can't see them, but they're my best friends."

"Oh, I see. Then there's nothing to worry about, is there?" he grinned, momentarily wiping the worry from his mind.

Suddenly, there was a knock at our door and Mama went to answer it. Our neighbor, Mr. Walker, in a state of panic, came past Mama into the living room, where my father and I sat. "Slim, you've got to come help me. The storm blew down one of my fences. The cattle have broken through and I can't find half of them. I'm in a terrible bind, and you're the only man around to help," he panted, trying to catch his breath, his face pale and drawn.

As soon as he entered our house I noticed a foul stench had followed him. I instinctively covered my nose and mouth with my hands, trying to fight the putrid smell quickly infiltrating our home. The smell was so bad I almost gagged with every breath, causing me to bury my nose even deeper into the palms of my hands. Not only was the smell alarming, but I noticed a strange movement in his stomach area, which was obscured by a dark brown haze. I looked at my mother and father to see if they had problems breathing, but they didn't seem to notice the horrible smell hanging around our neighbor, so I looked past the dark cloud that covered his stomach, wondering if perhaps this was the cause of the offending odor.

Much to my horror and surprise, the movement I had witnessed earlier took on the form of large coiling snakes. Their black scales caught the light and flashed blue and silver with every twisting movement of their writhing bodies. Our neighbor's stomach became a mass of these hideous creatures. They bit at him and each other, and were tearing large chunks of his flesh and body away with their constant chewing, devouring him bit by bit. I forgot the smell and began to scream, afraid that any second the vipers would jump out in search of new hosts, and attach themselves to myself or my family.

"Carol, what's the matter?" my father asked in astonishment, momentarily quieting my screams. "You know Mr. Walker, you don't have to be afraid of him."

From nowhere John's voice boomed in my head, "This is sickness, Carol. Look at it and understand it."

"What?" I questioned, but received no reply, realizing he had left me once again.

"Oh, Papa," I shouted, still looking at the pale man standing in front of me. "Mr. Walker is sick, it's his stomach. It's full of snakes. . . it's horrible!" I buried my head into my father's arm, not wanting to watch the twisting serpents consume the man standing only a few feet away, who shifted uneasily where he stood, the color now completely drained from his face.

"She's got a good imagination, Slim," Mr. Walker chuckled nervously, as he took off his hat and wiped his brow anxiously with a dirty bandana normally secured around his neck.

"She has a very big imagination," Papa replied uncertainly, patting me on the head.

"It's time for bed, Carol," my mother interjected sternly, as she walked past Mr. Walker to where I sat and grabbed my arm, pulling me off my father's lap and placing me securely next to her. "Tell Mr. Walker and your father good night," my mother instructed in a warning tone, and placed a firm hand on my shoulder.

"Good night, Papa. Good night, Mr. . ." I faltered, my voice trailing as I looked at the man in front of me.

I never did finish my sentence. As I started to speak to Mr. Walker, one of the larger snakes reared its ugly head and looked at me with its small dead eyes. It poised itself and made ready to strike. With a scream, I backed away from the monster and ran down the hall to my room, leaving the stench and snakes far behind.

That night the battlefield lay before me. Dark piles that I knew were not rocks or shrubs lay scattered from end to end. I looked at the heap of human carnage closest to me. His bloodied hands gripped a gun not unlike mine, and the metal of the barrel glittered ominously through the rising smoke. His features were distinguishable from where I stood, and I could see a small smile grace his boyish features. His hair was blond and a pale lock, the color of moonlight, spilled out from under his helmet and over his dirty forehead. His eyes were a clear blue. I followed his hollow stare upward into the sky, and I choked back a tear at what met my gaze. There between the clouds of death, created by man in his supreme stupidity, a single star winked against the dark heavens. My insignificance became absolute. I laughed at the ignorance of all mankind and wept for its folly.

"Get a hold of it," I chided myself, wiping back the tears running freely down my face. The sound of gunfire sobered me, and I began to plan a route across the littered field. I was the last of my platoon to leave this area. They had all left after the last barrage of enemy bombing had ended. I knew within moments, when the firing stopped again, the enemy would close in around me.

They were close. I could hear the snow crunching under their feet, and the twigs giving way as they snapped against the cold metal of enemy guns.

A massive explosion blasted near my right side. I realized

I had almost waited too long. I knew now, before the bombing started, was the time for me to run across the field and join my friends. I hunched over, pulling my upper body into a ball and started to run, zig-zagging my way across, tripping over pieces of human arms and legs as I advanced. Another orange blast ripped through the sky, catapulting spitting pieces of molten fire and lead furiously into the icy ground to my left, deforming dead bodies and silencing the moaning of the almost dead forever. The enemy soldiers had reached my previous hiding place and began to fire rounds of ammunition. The hum of machine guns became coupled with the sound of exploding bombs. The sound was deafening and added to my fear, tearing down any defenses I had, tugging at my already frayed nerves. Planes screeched overhead. I fell down on my belly and crawled in the cold snow, filling my mouth with ice and the blood of my comrades, which had collected in dark pools where they had been shot and murdered.

Only a few yards more and I would be safe. Only a few yards more, I told myself, leading myself on to believe I stood a chance. Out of nowhere I felt someone grab my leg. I turned and, using the blade of my bayonet, chopped off the hand at the wrist. The dying soldier looked at me in bewilderment, and then at the mutilation I had inflicted. He muttered something about my helping him, then fell face down in the snow. He became just another number, another fatality, like so many piled around him. I had killed many soldiers, but something inside of me finally snapped. I began to vomit. Blasts exploded all around me. I jumped up from my crawling position, covered in blood, snow, and vomit, and ran to where I could see my platoon only a few yards away. Suddenly a wave of bullets whizzed above my head. As my platoon retaliated, I was caught in the cross-fire.

"No!" I screamed, the word coming in a gasp and sob, and a hot searing pain ripped across my belly as iron tore into my flesh. I felt coils of my entrails spilling out onto the ground and I screamed again, grabbing at the life falling from my body. I tried to hold onto these looping pieces of what I once was, but staggered and fell into a pool of my own blood which was spreading in a crimson lake below me. I tried to mouth my objections to God and the world, but my voice was silenced. Only a gurgle of frothy blood dribbled over my lips, quieting my lifeless body forever.

"I'm dying. I'm dying. Oh, my God, I'm dying!" I tried to scream.

"Carol, you're fine. Wake up," my mother's soothing voice echoed from somewhere far away.

I finally awoke, protected in her warm embrace. I glanced around the room to make sure I wasn't caught in the throes of yet another nightmare. Only after I was certain I was awake, did a wave of relief wash over me. With my feeling of safety, however, came the painful memory of my nightmare, and I began to weep uncontrollably.

"There, there," my mother whispered, drying my tears. "Everything is alright."

"Yes, Mama," I whimpered, as she tucked me back into bed and kissed my forehead.

"I'll stay here until you fall asleep, Honey," she said. As the soft strains of a gospel tune began to fill my room, I fell into a forgetful sleep.

After the last breakfast plate was dried, I bounded out of the house. It was a beautiful morning, holding all the promise of a fairy tale, and I hurried to where John and Raa were waiting.

"Hello, Carol," John shouted in greeting as I approached.

"Hello, John," I answered, giving Raa a scratch on the head, getting a lick of his sandpaper tongue on my fingers in return. "Why did you leave last night?" I asked him, perturbed with his unexplained absence.

"I didn't leave," he snorted indignantly, beginning to walk away down the road from the house. I wasn't going to let him off so easily, so Raa and I followed him as he walked.

"You were the one who left, Carol, not me," he muttered.

"I did not, and you know it!" I snapped, a little angry that he would even suggest such a thing.

"There's an ugly red showing in your aura, Carol," he teased, and stopped walking as he looked down at me. "It's very unbecoming on you, you know."

That did it! I became furious with this man who first accused me of leaving, and then suddenly began to make fun of me. I decided that I didn't need his ridicule today, and without a word I turned and flounced away.

"Well, Raa, I guess Carol doesn't want to learn today," I heard John shouting loud enough for me to hear. I didn't respond but kept walking. "I suppose she knows everything there is to know, even about her dream and the hole behind her father. It must really be wonderful to know so much."

At the mention of my dream and father, I stopped dead in my tracks. Curiosity replaced my anger and I slowly turned around, looking back to where John and Raa stood. "Come on, Raa," John said with a dramatic sigh, patting Raa on the back, completely ignoring me. "We have a lot to do today, and we don't need to stay around someplace where we're not wanted. Come on, let's be going." He began to walk in the opposite direction from where I was standing.

"No, wait!" I yelled, running to them, as their forms began to vaporize into the air.

Luckily, as I ran closer to them, their forms became more solid, and were completely intact by the time I reached John's side. "Change your mind?" he asked with his impish grin, cupping my chin in his hand as looked into my eyes.

"Yes," I responded, and averted my eyes to the ground, completely cowed. "I'm sorry for being so mean, it's just that. . ."

"It's just that sometimes things don't happen or exist the way you think they do," John completed my sentence and let go of my chin. "Just be patient and always think of a place as a place for learning. Always be open to other people's ideas as well as your own, because sometimes the other people are right. And, Carol, do yourself and me a big favor. Don't say you're sorry. Sorry is a self-defeating word. Only undesirable things are considered "sorry" on this earth plane. Every time you say you are sorry, you are reinforcing an idea or thought that you are an undeserving being. This could not be further from the truth. Every being in this universe is perfect and most deserving. Apologize nicely, but don't say you are sorry, understand?"

"Yes, I do!" I replied happily.

"Good!" he exclaimed, giving me a light jovial slap on my back. "Let's go and sit by the oak tree, Carol. We have a lot to discuss today."

When everyone was comfortably sitting near the old oak tree, John began to speak. "To answer the question you recently asked, as to why I disappeared last night, I had no choice. You became worried and afraid of what you were seeing and experiencing. You became so involved in your own worry that it blocked everything else out, including me. Your connection was severed, and I couldn't get through. Your telephone was off the hook, so to speak. So, in fact, it wasn't I who left, but you."

"Alright, okay," I mumbled, feeling a little guilty that I had accused my friend of deserting me.

"Let's talk about that dream you keep experiencing over and over," John spoke softly. "You're dreaming about another life you had before this one. In that lifetime you were a soldier in Germany and a very angry, unhappy man. You were killed violently in that life and you were very afraid of death. You didn't take time to rest between that life and this life, so you carry the memory very strongly with you and that memory of your struggle of fear and death itself is bleeding through into your dreams. Once you work out your struggles within about death and your angers about that lifetime, you will stop dreaming about that other part of you."

I had a huge question mark on my face. "You mean we really don't die?" I asked, confused.

"We change form," he said. "When the cool weather of autumn is here the peach trees loose their leaves and they appear dead, but when you look closely at the trees, you can see the tree is very much alive and has peaches already set for the next bloom. We are much the same as that tree, we appear dead but we already have set within us the next life. That dream was your last experience before this one, that's all."

This felt right to me as I sat looking at the trees surrounding us. I felt very clear and peaceful after what John told me, like a very difficult puzzle had been solved and put away. As quickly as I put it away, the picture of my father, the black hole with the grave and tombstone, instantly filled my mind.

"I'm glad you asked," John replied out loud even though I had said nothing.

"You cheated!" I cried accusingly, vexed he had been mentally eavesdropping.

"Thoughts are energy, Carol, and you were thinking so loudly I couldn't help but hear you," he laughed defensively, while brushing an oak leaf off his overalls.

He reached down, took my small hand into his large one, and very quietly spoke. "The hole above your father's head is the bridge between this life and his next life. It's getting close to his time to leave this world and go to his next place in life. Death is supposed to be a happy time, Carol. That means his work here is finished. Let him go with love and that will help him on the spiritual path."

"No!" I screamed, recoiling away from him as if he were poison, and scrambled to my feet. "No, I don't believe you. And I don't want to let him go!"

"Carol," John began to say, but never had a chance to finish. Hot tears stung my cheeks as I ran away from the oak tree, leaving John and Raa behind. I ran blindly down the dirt road and past our house, into the cotton field where I knew my father was working. I couldn't believe what John had said. My father couldn't die, he just couldn't. I loved him more than anything in the world, and the thought of losing him was devastating.

Large white blossoms, the size of silver dollars, loomed above my head. The brambles scratched at my bare legs and tore against my face. Huge, striped bumble bees swarmed in a frenzy around me as I knocked the insects off the puffy blooms while I made my way across the field. I recognized my father from across the field and I called to him, tripping over the loose dirt clods beneath my feet. He was working near the irrigation ditch, and turned to me when he heard my voice. His coat, beneath the dirt, was blue plaid, under which he wore a shirt of red flannel. His pants were navy blue, and hung like a sack over his slim body. He took off his torn beige work gloves as I approached and squatted down, not wanting the dirt he always wore from head to toe to touch me with his embrace.

This was the hero of my life. This was the knight of all my fairy tales, and I knew without him in my world the castles would crumble away, leaving me only bitter reality and painful desolation as companions.

"Oh, Papa!" I cried, and held him in desperation, not ever wanting to let go.

"What is it, kitten?" he asked with concern, my tears now falling uncontrollably, soaking the dirt clinging to his jacket and turning it to mud.

"You can't die, Papa!" I pleaded, choking on my tears. "You can't die, I won't let you!"

"Now, who said I was going to die, Carol?" he responded thoughtfully, wiping the tears away from my face. "And even if I were to die, it's just another part of life. I'm not afraid of it, honey. I know that one of these days it will happen, and when it does, I'll be ready. Death, my little kitten, wears a smile, and not a frown as you may think. You're still young yet, but when you're my age you will understand. So, when I die don't be sad for me, but be happy and know that I'll be smiling down at you from Heaven."

"But not now. You can't go now," I begged, not swayed by what he had said.

"I'll have no choice when or how I'll go. It's all in the hands of God, and I believe he's a mite smarter than I am."

"But I love you so much, Papa," I said beseechingly, my tears now reduced to sniffles.

"And I love you, too. No matter what happens, always remember that," he ended and stood up, taking my small hand into his as we walked back toward the house.

I realized that I had picked up a rock in my shoe when I had been running, and we stopped as I unfastened the lace, holding onto my father for support. An unsteady dirt clod caught me off balance and I stepped down, my foot bare, to steady myself from falling. A hot pain suddenly tore into the bottom of my foot and I screamed and jumped away from it instantly. My father quickly grabbed me into his strong arms, and I looked down and saw the fragmented body of a bumble bee fall from my foot to the ground. I screamed again as the pain of the sting increased. My foot began to swell. I could feel the poison spreading up from my foot to my leg. My father ran with me in his arms, through the field and to the house. He shouted for my mother to open the door and sat me in his chair as my crying intensified. He grabbed a pair of tweezers from the bathroom and pulled out the offending stinger, while my mother mixed a poultice of cornstarch and water to cover the wound.

After everything had been attended to my crying subsided. My brothers' curiosity was satisfied as each one checked in to see what had happened, and soon left again. My father stayed with me, and rocked me in his arms, as we sat comfortably in his chair. He murmured soothing words to me and stroked my hair, as my mother busily prepared our dinner.

I was at peace and happy for the first time all day, and I welcomed the warm tranquility of my home. I looked above my father's head one more time, as I was falling into a quiet slumber. I noticed that instead of the black hole gaping so predominantly behind him, a soft rosy glow filled the room where he sat. I smiled then, with the knowledge we were protected in a cloud of love where death was an impossibility and very far away.

I awoke to the sound of Mrs. Walker talking to my mother as she entered our house. In my state of grogginess, I could hear my mother trying to calm Mrs. Walker down. At the mention of my name, I perked up, now fully conscious, and turned to where the two women stood. My father, I noticed, was already watching with interest. "Now settle down and tell me what is going on, Mary," my mother advised, wearing an expression of concern.

"It's Joel," she rambled excitedly. "He's sick. He was fine until this morning, when all of a sudden he fell over and grabbed his stomach. He's been in bed moaning ever since. I haven't been able to leave him until now. We had to fetch the doctor early this morning!"

I winced at the mention of his stomach. It brought back the memories of last night when I had seen the snakes chewing away at his entrails. "Now, what's this you were saying about Carol?" my mother continued, putting the bits and pieces of the frantic woman's story together.

"You know!" Mrs. Walker smirked accusingly, pointing a finger at where I sat in the chair. "Joel told me. You were here last night when your daughter told him he was sick. I find it strange that he was healthy until then." She turned to look at my mother. Her eyes narrowed and burned with a piercing light. "I appreciate all you've done for us, but we are God-fearing people, so we won't be visiting here anymore. Especially now that we know your daughter's a . . .a witch!"

"A what?" my father and mother both gasped in astonishment, shock paralyzing them where they stood.

"A witch!" she screamed, and crossed herself hurriedly as she ran through the door into the inky blackness of the night, as if the devil himself were at her heels. I could hear the door slam behind my father as he followed the woman in hot pursuit.

The cry of a newborn

Loud - Strong

The cry of Life

Growth - Work - Strife

The calm of Death

Work - Complete

From the Shadows of Earth
to the
sight of Soul

The calm of Death

Love Peace Joy

CHAPTER THREE

Death

"I don't care what you say, Slim. It's just not natural and I don't like it. At first I didn't pay much attention to it, but now it's gotten out of hand," I heard my mother say, her voice carrying down the short hall from the living room where she was sitting with my father.

"Oh, Jewell, there's nothing to worry about," my father protested calmly.

"There isn't, is there?" my mother replied, raising her voice to a high strained pitch. "You call what's been happening nothing?"

'It's coincidence, that's all," my father explained.

"Hogwash, Slim. I don't accept it as being coincidence," she snorted, the floorboards creaking in protest as she began to pace along the floor. "First Joel Walker gets sick and dies. Then Carol tells a woman in town that she'll have a baby boy even before she had conceived."

"What's so unnatural about a woman having a baby?" my father laughed, only adding to my mother's anger. "You had nine yourself!"

"But she was over forty and she did have a boy!" my mother screeched, ignoring my father's last comment. "And now to top it all, Carol can't talk about anything except for you dying."

"I'm fine, Jewell," my father replied, his voice tinged with uncertainty.

"Thank our dear Lord for that," she snapped, "but I don't like what's happening, Slim. I don't like it one bit!"

I closed the door of my bedroom, which I shared with my brothers, and quietly tip-toed back to the warmth of my bed. Every night for the last few months, it was always the same. My mother, usually so warm and kind, steered clear of me, regarding me as a freak, an unnatural spawn of the Devil. She never came right out and said it, but then, she didn't have to. I already knew. Only my father, and of course my brother David, came to my defense. I spent most of my time with John, Raa, my father, and my brother.

My father and I became closer as each day passed. In the afternoons, when he finished work for the day, he would come home and I would be the first to greet him. I came to enjoy this time of day more than any other. In the evenings when my mother would usually be busy preparing dinner, my father had a habit of lying on the sofa while I would massage his back, neck and head. During this time I felt myself becoming two people: on one hand I remained myself while on the other I became a lovely Egyptian woman, clad all in purple and green veiling. For what seemed like hours, everyday I would work over him and he would fall into a quiet sleep. I knew through this ancient custom, I was preparing him somehow, reworking and balancing his energy. I noticed as I worked over him, a subtle arrangement of his energy was taking place, a shifting of the inner and outer energy. I was not only massaging his physical body, but his emotional and astral bodies as well. I was connecting these other bodies with his soul or higher self, encompassing all four aspects of his being, giving balance and wholeness to his state of perfect being.

His energy began to shift from around his feet to his shoulders and head, connecting him to his higher self in a beautiful hue of the clearest blue. I could see his spiritual values were becoming more predominate, more important as the days passed. I no longer felt any sadness or remorse, just a quieting feeling of acceptance and joy. I realized that my father wasn't leaving me, only taking a journey to a place of learning and perfect universal love. I knew from John's teachings that only his form was changing not his essence.

Yes, these four individuals were my family and were the ones who loved and accepted me for what I was. My father told me I had been given a gift from God. My brother was only amused by what I had to say. John, on the other hand, when I questioned him, told me it was neither a gift or anything funny. He said I was merely a student of self. An individual who, like a knight of old, was on a quest. A quest for knowledge, nothing more. I liked John's explanation the most. As I drifted off to sleep, blocking out the argument in the next room, I tried to visualize myself riding a beautiful white stallion, holding a fluttering banner of gold and purple and riding off in the King's name to accomplish some great and impossible task, one in which I would invariably succeed.

My polished armor glitters in the golden sunshine and the cheers of adoring villagers fill my ears. I wait until the shouts subside and pledge to defend them from every foe. I hold my lance beside me and charge through the throng, off to some far away mountain where a dragon scourges the countryside. Finally, the mist of dreams gathers around me and I ride to a place where sleep is kind and filled with peace.

Instantly, I found myself walking along a dirt road. The sun had recently set behind a jagged ridge of towering, purple mountains, painting the sky a bloody red. Twilight had darkened the heavens behind and above me, causing the mountains to become a dark silhouette against the burning horizon. A solitary star shot across the sky. Silver glitter trailed quietly behind it, then dissolved with the star into nothingness. I made a silent wish and continued walking down the road. Soon, far off in the distance, I could distinguish two headlights of an approaching car. My pulse began to quicken as it traveled closer to me, the hum of the engine quickly turning into a roar.

Without knowing why, I jumped into the middle of the road. I had to stop the car. I had to tell them it was necessary for them to change directions. I waved to them frantically, but they didn't seem to notice, just continued racing toward me.

"Stop!" I screamed, the car now only a few yards away as I began to back away from my vulnerable position. Still the car advanced. I began to run, but the car was already upon me. I stumbled and covered my eyes, a huddled mass in the middle of the road, and waited for the driver to change his current path. I prayed that the driver of the car would see me as I uncovered my eyes and stared at the green metal monstrosity speeding toward me. The tires screeched as the driver saw me and hit his brakes, the momentum fish-tailed the car side to side.

The car was now so close that I could distinguish the face of the driver. I shouted again when I saw it was my father who sat behind the wheel. Just as the car was about to hit me with its force, it veered to the left, leaving me safe and untouched. The sudden movement from its intended path catapulted the speeding automobile end-over-end, smashing it into a mangled heap of metal where it rested on its side, a macabre work of art dedicated to destruction. I ran to the car and looked inside. There, amid the twisted metal and smoke, lay my father. A gentle smile played on his lips as he looked tenderly into my eyes.

"It's alright, kitten," he said comfortingly. "I've seen where I am going and it's more beautiful than you could ever imagine. Just always remember that I love you very much." Saying that, he closed his eyes, the picture faded, and I once again slipped into a quiet darkness.

"What do you think?" John inquired the next morning, raising an eyebrow questioningly when I had finally reached him at our special place by the wood pile.

"What do you mean?" I said, worried. I was already aware this discussion was leading to the topic of my father.

"Everyday for the past year, you have been working with changing and restructuring energy. You have been smoothing it out, so to say, creating a bridge from this dimension to the next, preparing your father for his spiritual journey from this life to the next, enabling him to let go of physical aspects that he needs to leave behind on this earth plane. Without this preparation on the earth plane, some souls have a hard time crossing over. They become confused and frightened because no one seems to pay them any attention on the physical level. They are caught in a limbo of their own creation and live in a world between the two worlds of flesh and spirit. Sadly enough, they don't know they have died and spend countless years in a frustrated state of being. I am pleased with what you have been doing, Carol, and I wanted you to understand the impact of your work. You have consciously and subconsciously been cleaning out and restructuring your father's energy around his head and shoulders through daily massage. The hole represents the bridge or area where he had already elected to make the transition. You made his preparation for death complete. He is now ready to die."

With John's last words, I knew he was right. I had seen his consciousness shifting and found that I actually had known this for some time. I knew it was only a matter of time, but suddenly I missed my father greatly and I began to cry. I wasn't crying for him because I knew where he was going, but for myself, a little girl who would miss her father.

"When will he die?" I questioned, wiping away the tears staining the fabric of my dress like raindrops.

"It has already begun, Carol," John replied.

I jumped to my feet, rubbed the tears from my eyes, and began to run in the direction of the house.

"Where are you going?" I heard John shout from behind.

"To find my father," I yelled, without turning back to where I knew John stood.

"Let him go, Carol. Let him go," I heard John's voice ringing in my head.

"I will!" I shouted over my shoulder aloud. "But not until I hug him and tell him not to worry. Everything will be alright."

"Yes, Carol, it will be," he answered in a faint whisper. Then he disappeared just as quickly as he had come.

I could hear my father's voice in the distance mingled with shouts of excitement from a few of my brothers.

I hadn't slowed my pace as I rounded the back of the house to the front, where the commotion seemed to be originating. But I stopped in my tracks when I discovered the source of their excitement. It took all of my strength to keep my legs steady beneath me as I approached my father.

For there, in our front yard, was the center of my dream. The car was green and had been polished to a high luster, mirroring my father's figure. The grill sparkled with chrome and broke into a welcoming grin. Its headlights, which I remembered so vividly, stared at me, conveying knowledge and understanding of the near future.

"What do you think, Kitten?" my father proudly asked, patting the hood of the car as I neared.

The sight of my father standing next to his impending destiny was overpowering, but acceptance overcame my fear and I shot him a bright smile.

"It's just fine," I responded, giving the shiny car a pat of unspoken comprehension. "Do you know how to work it?"

"I was born to drive this car," my father exclaimed triumphantly, bringing squeals of excitement from my brothers who were now pushing each other into the car.

"Yes Carol, he was born for this," John's voice interjected. "He knows what he needs to do."

"Yes Papa, I suppose you were," I replied, hugging him around his waist, "but no matter what happens, know I'll always love you more than anything."

"I know that, kitten," he smiled as he picked me up into his strong arms.

I held onto him perhaps for the last time, memorizing the feel of his body next to mine. I breathed in deeply his masculine scent. A sweet mingling of the earth and living, growing things. I held onto that moment for as long as I could, until my mother called us all into the house. With a tender kiss, he sat me back onto the ground as we all filed into the house for breakfast. For the whole family, this was a day filled with anticipated excitement of rides in the new car.

The day dawned like any other. Golden sunlight streamed through all of the open windows in the house, lighting each room brightly with a natural glow. Although it was only ten o'clock in the morning, the heat was already sweltering, especially in the kitchen where my mother and I were busy canning fat, plump peaches.

My mother, every so often, blotted her forehead with her apron, catching the beads of perspiration which steadily ran from her brow down her flushed cheeks. I decided to forego my apron and wiped the offending drops away with my sticky hands, getting more of the jam on myself than into the green tinted glass jars sitting in orderly lines on the table in front of me.

"You haven't said much today," my mother said as she swatted away a large black fly.

"No, I guess I haven't," I mustered with a small shrug of my shoulders.

I was pensive for a reason, and my mother of all people wasn't the one I wanted to tell why. I knew my father wasn't coming home tonight. I had known it since yesterday. Actually, he wasn't ever coming home again. I had hugged him for the last time this morning when he and my brothers went to pick grapes for extra spending money. Even though I understood the concept of death, I began to cry as they drove away. Not out of fear, but sadness, out of a sense of personal loss. I loved him above all others in my family, but I was trying to be strong and do as John had told me last night.

"In love, life, or death it is the same," John had said.

"You must release your father to his highest good. Too often we hold back and onto others to satisfy our own private needs, forgetting that we may be hurting those we love the most by denying them their right to freedom and happiness."

"Day-dreaming again, Carol?" my mother inquired as she poured the last of the hot wax onto the top of a peach-filled jar, sealing in the fragrant juices.

"Yes, I guess I was," I replied, the cheerful smile on my face belying the pensive look in my eyes.

"Well, pay attention to what you're doing. I don't want you cutting yourself on the lids before you tighten them down," she replied, agitated.

My mother was gradually becoming anxious and worried. The black streak in her aura was now glaringly predominate against the mustard color above her head. I knew this time she had a good reason, unlike her usual misdirected state of worry.

Mama sat a large metal tub on the kitchen floor and began to fill it with soapy water. "Carol," she said turning to look at me, "go out to the shed and bring in some of these large jars." She lifted a half-gallon jar as a sample of the size she needed.

I hurried out the back door into the bright noon sunlight. As I scurried to the old shed, I felt the sun hot on my back and saw my shadow cast directly out in front of me, the elongated inky black reflection of me followed my every step.

John's voice spoke to me inside my head, "Look at your shadow, Carol." I stopped short of my mission to look into the shadow in front of me. There I saw a dark yellowish-red color, almost a rusty yellow-red. "Carol, you're full of worry and concern about your father and brothers. It is showing in your aura," John's soft, stern voice again entered my thoughts.

I silently agreed as I watched the colors radiate about my shadow. After I reached the shed and fetched the necessary jars, I started the short jaunt back to the house, thinking about the colors in my shadow the whole way.

Mama had finished filling the tub and the soapy water created a small sea of sparkling foam which caught the light every time Mama put another jar into the tub. "Carol, you have just the right size hands for this job, so you get to play in the water while you clean out each one of these jars," Mama said as she handed me a wash cloth. Normally, I would've thought it fun to play in the large tub of soapy water, pretending to be the captain of a fleet of ships, the jars being my submarines. But today my heart and mind were not into the task. And as a result, I moved slowly and quietly cleaning the jars one by one, thoughts of my family pre-occupied my actions. I vaguely heard my mother's voice singing to herself one of her favorite songs, "That Old Ragged Cross".

"Carol, you're awfully quiet and deep in thought today, what's wrong?" she stopped singing to ask me.

Without thinking I answered, 'I'm worried about the car crash." I immediately regretted my words as I watched her features grow dark.

"You stop thinking like that or I'm going to take a stick to you!" she scolded, angry, "Now, stop it, do you hear me?"

"Yes, Mama," I said, subdued. But no matter how hard I tried, I couldn't push the thought away.

After the last jar was rinsed clean and boiled in the large steaming pots, the ripe fruit was ready for canning. In the meantime, Mama peeled and cut the peaches. I watched her hands, quick and agile with experience, scoop out each nutty pit, leaving a ruby red hole in the center of each flesh colored peach half.

"Carol," she said over her shoulder, her eyes never leaving her work, "I have another job for you. Isn't it nice how God makes jobs just right for each person?" It was more a statement than a question, because without waiting for an answer she continued, "Take your little hands and pack the peach halves down real tight into the jars and get all of the air out from between the peaches. A job made to order for you!"

Her cheeriness seemed like a facade to me, covering her true worry and concern. I wanted to ask her, "Don't you care? Aren't you afraid for Papa and the boys?" But I knew any talk of the crash would only upset her and bring about a verbal thrashing on her part. She made it perfectly clear that there was to be no talk of "nonsense", as she called it, about my foretelling the future. So I went about my new job silently, a sense of dread for my father and brothers overwhelmed me.

Suddenly, John appeared right in front of me. He stood there, piercing my eyes with his straightforward gaze. "Carol," he said, "look at what your doing. Your worry and concern is like asking for the thing your concerned about to happen. It's like taking all your mixed up colors and dousing your family with them." His voice turned stern as he said, "Change that right now. Even the peaches you are canning will have a bad taste because of your bad energy. If you change your thoughts you can help your family. Imagine your brothers as safe and happy. Picture them in your mind's eye all shining in a golden light. The color gold filters out all negative energy. Now see your brothers, in the new car, all wrapped in golden light. See them happy and excited, as they were when they left this morning. Picture the air turning golden inside the car." He pointed to the packed plump peaches in the jars on the counter. "See them golden, like the peaches in those jars. See it all aglow now, see the outside around the car turn golden."

"But John," I wailed silently, "I'm still having a hard time."

John stopped his instructions to look at me a moment. He looked through me, he looked inside of me, he looked around me. "I can see the problem, Carol, your aura is still a rusty color. Let's clean you out first and then start over again."

All of a sudden I saw golden specks floating around me, dazzling in their brilliance of yellow-gold light. Then I felt myself become golden light all aglow.

"Now put your family in the car, the car inside a golden balloon, and let them float out of sight. Feel happy for them," John said in a soothing voice.

This time it was much easier to visualize. Every time the car came to mind I saw the golden balloon floating away in the light breeze. I started to sing a song of my own, under my breath at first, then quietly stronger as the words soothed my aching heart.

"My balloon is golden and bright, flowing in safety out of sight . . ." I sang softly. The afternoon went quickly, as I played this new game and sang my song.

The sound of an approaching car alerted my mother, and she ran to open the front door while I trailed silently behind. The headlights of the car illuminated the living room in two streams of unnatural light, catching the frozen figure of my mother in its beam. Like a terrified animal, she stood motionless until the car stopped and the lights were extinguished. I listened for familiar sounds, but heard none. I didn't expect any. I knew and understood what John was trying to tell me. It was very clear what was happening. If not to my mother, then to me. A small moan escaped her throat as the figure of a tall man climbed out of the car. He held his worn hat in his hand as he slowly walked toward us.

With her face and eyes fixed on the approaching figure, my mother gave a whimper like that of a child and grabbed my hand into hers. I could feel her body trembling and then sway as we recognized the man as one of our neighbors who had gone working with my father and brothers early this morning.

"Evenin', Jewell," he said, clearing his throat, his voice

hoarse and laced with grief.

"Evenin'," my mother replied in a strained voice, adding politely, "Won't you come in?"

"Thank you," he replied, shuffling into the living room as he nervously fumbled with his old felt hat.

We followed slowly behind him, where he stood in the middle of the living room, facing away from us. His shoulders and head were bent as if he were carrying a heavy weight on his large back.

"Tell me," my mother said, her features taut and ashen.

The man heaved a heavy sigh, and turned to where we stood. In his eyes he wore a haunted look, framed with lids red and raw, the obvious product of recent crying.

"Jewell, I'm not very good at this sort of thing," he choked, holding back the tears, "so I'll just tell you straight out. Slim was killed in an auto accident today. The boys are in the hospital, but they'll be just fine. I'm sorry to have to tell you this, Ma'am, since I've never been one for pretty speeches, but Slim was the finest man I ever knew. I'll take you to the hospital to see the boys as soon as you're ready," he finished and walked out the door. We could hear his sobs through the screen door as he waited near his car.

My mother stood perfectly still in shocked silence. She didn't blink. She didn't move. She almost didn't breathe, until after some moments she let go of my hand and ordered me to get our sweaters.

Although the weather was hot and I knew sweaters weren't necessary, I did as she told me and immediately returned to where she still stood, her eyes staring blankly at my father's chair.

"Come, Carol," she stated, gently taking her sweater from my arms, "your father and brothers have need of me."

On the way to the hospital, I was dropped off at our neighbor's house. Under normal circumstances, I would be thrilled to stay there. The house was always warm and cozy. The furniture was old, but beautiful and smelled of beeswax polish. And by far the greatest thing about our neighbor lady's house was the large sugar cookies she baked. The aroma always filled the house, making the mouth water, fulfilling every childhood fantasy.

But I wasn't hungry. I wasn't even interested in exploring the house or sitting on the pretty furniture. I felt out of place and a little bit lonely. I sought the solitude of the outdoors where I was free from any human sorrow, and away from the restrictions of human dwellings. Instead, I breathed in deeply the warm night air, sweet with the scent of wild flowers and hay. I looked up above me and saw the pale sliver of a crescent moon high above the horizon, flanked by millions of sparkling stars.

I could hold back no longer, and as the tears invaded my eyes, my body began to rack with uncontrollable sobbing. All I could think was, John lied to me. He told me to use golden light around the car and my family, and I did, but look what happened anyway. He blatantly lied to me and I believed he was my best friend. I cried with the urgency that only one who has lost deeply can cry. The pain overtook any other emotion and I sat outside for a long while, experiencing that pain, the pain of the whole family.

Finally, when my crying had ceased to small sniffles, Mrs. Jones came outside to where I sat. I didn't know how long she had been waiting in the shadows, probably keeping a watchful eye out for the little girl who just lost her father. She took my hand and led me gently back into the house.

Once inside the tiny guest room I was completely familiar with, she overtook my feeble attempts to undress myself and got me ready for bed, tucked me in, and tenderly kissed me goodnight. Once I was safely in bed, covers pulled completely over my head, I escaped my sorrow into a sound sleep.

The murmuring of voices woke me the next morning, and as soon as I opened my eyes, the pain and hurting of last night came rushing back to me in twofold. I lay there letting the sharp daggers of my father's death twist and tear at my heart, listening to the muffled conversation from the kitchen as it drifted into my room.

"Jewell said it was a miracle anyone lived through that car crash," Mr. Jones said. "A car ran right through a stop sign and almost cut Slim's car in half. The boys are all okay, Slim's the only one who didn't make it. It's just a blessing from God they weren't all killed."

"Poor Jewell," Mrs. Jones replied. "What's she going to do without Slim? Slim was such a good—." She saw me enter the kitchen right then and stopped mid sentence. "Carol, you're up," she said, replacing what she was about to say about my father. "How about some breakfast?"

She took my silence to mean yes, and went about fixing me up a plate of warmed pancakes from the oven. Everything seemed to move in slow motion that day. Even the syrup, although warm, was taking its time spreading over the flaky stack. I ate slowly, and after what seemed like years, finished breakfast and went outside to play.

Usually, the Jones' huge fig tree in the back yard was my favorite climb, but not today. Not even the coercing whisper of the fig leaves could beckon me into its arms. Today I wanted to hide under the weeping willow. Its sweeping, melancholy leaves most appropriately fit my mood. I just wanted to be alone, I didn't even wish for John or Raa to be around me. I already missed my father, and this feeling of loneliness penetrated the core of my being. The pain came in waves, washing over me first strong, then breaking and mellowing out to seem not as severe. Those times when I wasn't in complete pain for my father, my mother's stare would haunt me and bring me more grief. I couldn't stop myself from thinking, did I in some way cause all this to happen? I could tell by the look on my mother's face last night and by the energy she threw at me like a sharp-pointed dart, that she felt I was guilty. Maybe, just maybe, she was right. The pain hurt every fiber in my body. Even my aura ached, it felt like the fragile shell of an egg mercilessly cracked open.

I laid under the weeping willow in my bed of pain for most of the afternoon. Then I looked up and noticed John and Raa peering at me through the dense foliage. "John!" I cried. "You're here! You and Raa are here for me, I've felt so alone," forgetting my earlier wish of not wanting to see the pair.

John smiled. "Carol, you're alone because you wanted to be alone. You want to feel your pain, and it's okay to feel pain," he said. "Now let's put that energy to better use."

"What do you mean, John?" I asked, confused. "What better use?"

"Well, we can help in healing your family, for one thing," he said. "And we can help your father over and you can talk to him and know he is always with you."

"Oh, sure John," I said in disbelief. I was skeptical about anything he had to say. "You said the golden light would help and lied about that, didn't you? And now you want me to play these games again? No thank you."

John reached his hand out to me. His grasp felt warm and understanding. "Carol, the energy you wrapped your brothers in worked. They lived through that terrible crash with just a few cuts and bruises," he said, then his voice became stern. I knew that voice well, it was his no-nonsense voice. "Now stop feeling sorry for yourself and let's talk to your father and help him on over to a peaceful, loving place."

I stopped and thought for a moment. He was right.

Everyone was okay and I knew my father was going to die. I sighed a defeated sigh and said, "Okay John, show me how to help."

"This is what we need to do with your father. Simply visualize him Carol, and go to where he is," John instructed.

Suddenly John and I stood in a place filled with light. The light was golden in color and I felt pleasantly warm all over, though I knew instinctively the light gave off no heat. My father stood near the center of the light, flanked on either side by beings of brilliant golden light. My father was smiling at me and I heard his words of greeting and love. I had never felt such happiness. My heart swelled with sublime ecstasy as I told my father in thought how much I loved him.

"I know," he replied sweetly. "I love you too, my daughter, but it's time for me to go."

"Release him, Carol, to his highest good," John instructed.

I knew what John said was true and I did what he asked of me with joy.

"In my love, I release you my father," I stated, "and I ask your higher guides to help you move through the light of divine love."

He smiled at me once again and, nodding to his higher guides standing near him, moved through the light, passing from our view.

After that time I no longer felt any remorse. My father knew I loved him and existed in a place filled with love and happiness. I could wish for him now a greater paradise than this.

The days after my father's death passed quickly. Relatives I had never met before poured in from neighboring states to console my mother and express their sympathies at the funeral. John appeared from time to time, keeping me busy with lessons and helping me work with my father by letting go and seeing the golden light of love around him and my whole family.

"Carol, remember how you learned to play with the balloon and golden light before the car accident, and how it helped to protect your brothers from getting seriously hurt?" John asked me the day of the funeral. There was a particularly large group of relatives crowding into our home, coming in and out all day long bearing food and offers to help my mother through this difficult time.

"Yes," I replied, thinking about the day I consoled my

own fears with the golden light and balloon game.

"Well, I have another idea for you. I want you to do the same thing with your house and all the people coming and going for the next couple of days. This will help your family filter out all the hurt and lost feelings of your father's death as well as help you to release some of your own pain." He lowered his voice when he said the next sentence, even though no one but myself could hear him. "Make this your special game and don't tell anyone what you're doing."

"Why not?" I whispered back, one conspirator to another.

"Because when you talk about what you are doing others may not understand and start to make fun of you. Once that happens, you will begin to doubt yourself and the process, which will take all the power and fun out of it," he answered.

I used my imagination to picture our house filled with golden energy. I took this energy out and around the house, all the way to the driveway. I imagined everyone in the house breathing in the golden light, and I felt a sense of calmness within the house.

While sitting in the chair, imagining all this golden calmness, Peter's voice broke my concentration. His calls to Mark were faint, coming from the outdoors, but persistent. I went outside to see what was up.

"What are you doing?" I asked the two boys, talking to their backsides, since they were both lying on their stomachs looking under the house.

"Jip's under the house," Peter said, in a muffled voice. "He won't come out to eat or play or anything." Although Jip was the family dog, willing to give each of us kids equal attention, he was most loyal to Papa. We always considered him "Papa's dog" without hesitation.

Now Mark was trying to crawl under the wooden planks of the house to reach Jip. "Darn, I won't fit, he's too far back there." Both he and Peter crawled back out and began to brush the dirt off of themselves.

"Jip! Jip!" we all called in unison. Nothing happened.

"He'll come out when he gets hungry enough," I said finally, taking one last peek underneath the house just in case. We moved back into the house and I decided to resume my sitting in the living room. This time I chose a corner chair to observe my surroundings. Sadness shocked my body inside and out. I never felt anything so strong before, and all at one time, too.

"Carol, that's how all these people feel," John said in my inner-ear. "Use the color and light again."

I thought of a new game as I watched more people coming and going. In my mind's eye I imagined blowing up a huge balloon filled with the golden light. I puffed a breath of golden sparkling light into the balloon and watched it grow bigger and bigger. Then when it was just about to burst, I let the balloon go and watched it swoosh about the room, in a frenzied release of energy, spreading the golden light every-where as it swooped back and forth letting out all the air. I watched the effects this golden light had on the people I would let the balloon out on. Aunt Faye stopped short of what she was doing, as if she felt the change in her energy field. Others barely reacted at all, and those people I knew had a more stubborn air about them. They seemed not as sad but nor were they completely changed either, not like Aunt Faye.

That night most of the people went home and us kids went to bed. I fell into an exhausted sleep but not before listening to a grieving Jip underneath the bedroom, crying and whimpering in his own sad way.

The next day the house was again full of people, mostly relatives who had driven a far distance to see us. All that day I played with the light, especially enjoying the balloon game. I liked to watch it swoosh its light all over the room, sometimes only swooshing one person if that person was crying.

Again I tried to coax and plead Jip out from under the

house. I held out scraps of food I knew were his favorite, but he wouldn't budge. The only response I got was a whimpering noise, hurting and sad. I blew up one more balloon in Jip's honor and sent it under the house to him. I watched it release its golden light all over him. His whimpering ceased for a bit when I did that.

That same night the family was awakened by his howling several times. His howling was so forlorn and empty, I knew he missed Papa as much as I did. It hurt all over again to hear his incessant mourning.

One day the whimpers ceased. We knew Jip had finally joined his master.

I asked John why the dog made this choice.

"Animals exist on all dimensions," he replied as he, Raa and I sat under the shade of a mighty oak tree. "Where we exist, they do also. Some animals, like Jip or Raa, attach themselves to one particular person to act as their guide and friend. These little brothers and sisters are always drawn back lifetime after lifetime to that one individual person. If not in a physical form then in a spiritual one."

"So Raa is my friend forever?" I asked with interest, scratching the big cat between the ears.

"Yes, he made that choice back in a lifetime you shared in India," John said. "You had been hunting together among the trees and inadvertently startled a herd of elephants. They began to stampede, knocking you to the ground. You were trampled and killed instantly. Raa, much like your dog, stayed to protect your body until he starved and also died. This act cemented your combined karma and future life incarnations. Raa is here to guide you and keep you from danger of any sort. Everyone has an animal guide and they should treat these souls as the precious treasures from God they truly are."

That night I easily fell into a deep dream-filled slumber. I found myself walking, in full German dress uniform, down the isle of a large cathedral. People, crammed into the wooden benches, were dressed in somber blacks and greys. The sobs of weeping women filled the air and echoed high up into the domed and painted ceiling. Many men, I saw from their uniforms, were German soldiers of various ranks. Their familiar faces were drawn taut and expressionless. I followed their stern gazes to the altar of the church where a casket, covered with the Nazi flag, rested amid a sea of multi-colored, hot-house flowers. No one seemed to notice me as I walked up to where the body lay instated. I recognized the dead soldier immediately and I caught my breath. I might as well have been looking into a mirror. There, as if resting in a deep sleep, was the exact replica of myself. The mud and gore had been lovingly wiped away, exposing the handsome features of a very young and proud man. Too proud perhaps, and angry I mused, as I looked down at my quiet double. Without warning the cathedral disappeared into darkness as the casket began to glow with an unnatural light. No longer was I Carl experiencing Carl, but once again Carol. The body in the casket rose to a sitting position as it began to change form. I began to back away in fright from the coffin as the figure completed its process of transformation.

Slowly, the body gelled and I could distinguish the familiar features of my father. His face was expressionless except for the warmth filling his eyes. He rose his arm and pointed his forefinger in my direction as a swirl of golden light surrounded him, encased him, until his features were no longer discernible. For only a few seconds the shimmering light remained above the casket, until it, too, gradually disappeared into darkness.

I woke the next morning with the vision of my father freshly implanted in my mind. I knew this had been a message of love. He now understood what I had told him and had made an effort to reach me, giving me comfort and reassurance.

"Thank you, Papa," I said out loud as I sat alone in bed. "I love you, too."

Think and feel my presence near

to rise up above the World of doubt and fear

find that place where all is still

stand in this presence without fear

Spirit is here

Live in the very soul of spirit

where there is no

doubt or fear —

CHAPTER FOUR

Spirits

The afternoon sun was hot, but it didn't matter. I was too entranced by the surrounding countryside to give the heat much thought. Lush, green hills encircled us in the valley and sat securely tucked below the vast, towering mountain lining the horizon. Thousands of tiny wildflowers, painted in various hues of bright colors, danced amid the short prairie, rolling in unison with each new gust of warm wind. The sweeping motion of the wind-blown landscape pointed in the direction we were traveling and seemed to be welcoming us to our new life and home. Birds trilled from enormous weeping willow trees lining the banks of fast rushing creek beds which gurgled cheerfully in greeting as we drove up one of the first small hills to our new home.

On first sight of the house, I could do no more than stare. It was more beautiful than any of my mother's descriptions. There sitting on top of the hill, our hill, it sat in grand majesty. Holding court, in its regal splendor, as a monarch would in the center of several surrounding buildings.

My eyes quickly darted to these other buildings. From where I sat in the truck, I could see three log barns and a lovely white chicken house where cackling hens and roosters scratched in the nearby yard. There were several workshops and a beautiful old sawmill which sat down the road a couple hundred feet, nestled on the side of a creek bed, under the lush canopy of an old, gnarled guardian willow.

My uncle stopped the truck in front of the house. I looked over at my mother who sat next to me in the truck, her face glowed in rapt silence. Usually care-ridden with work and worry, her face seemed to be washed clean of any frustrations and was lit with a serene happiness I hadn't seen her wear in years. My brothers, who by this time had already climbed out of the back of the truck and its large, inclosed truck bed, were shouting with excitement as they ran the short distance to the house.

My uncle broke the silence in the truck cab where we sat as he opened the door and climbed out onto the dirt driveway. He slammed the door shut before walking around the truck to open the door on the side where my mother was sitting.

"Well, Jewell, ya done good," he said with a grin, his excitement hard to conceal as he opened the door and helped my mother out of the truck.

"We'll see," she said, the familiar worry creeping back into her voice, dampening her former feelings of joy. "We'll see." She then turned to me. "Come along, Carol."

"Yes, Mama," I replied automatically, too enraptured with the picture of our new home to add anything else.

I climbed out of the truck after my mother and stood where I was for some time, watching my uncle and mother disappear into the doorway of the house. I wanted the extra time alone to drink in the beauty of the structure.

The house was painted a stately white with a covered porch running the length of the house exuding the charm of an era long past gone. I could almost picture the figures of well-bred ladies in long silk skirts and gentlemen dandies in fashionable straw panama hats seated there, sipping cool lemonades on some long, hot afternoon. Lattice work had been artistically tucked beneath the wide porch roof and arched gracefully between the sturdy support posts anchored every few feet into the ground. Above the porch covering perched the second story. Two large french-paned windows rested beneath gabled and shingled dormers, causing them to look like large entreating eyes which welcomed me to enter.

In all honesty, this beautiful new house was not what I had expected. My mother, after returning home from the land purchase, had said our new home was beautiful but this place was a virtual castle compared to what we left behind, not to mention the land and surrounding buildings. Our old place may have been no more than a shanty, but it still had been our home. It was where I had grown up and been happy. Not to say I wouldn't be happy here. Happy was probably an understatement, but my roots were still firmly planted in my former home where memories of my father were still fresh in my mind, giving me unlimited strength and joy. And where dealing with my mother was concerned, strength was what I needed most of all.

In the past few years since my father's death, her attitude toward me had changed considerably. It had gone steadily from bad to worse. Somehow, I think, she blamed me for his death and felt I was responsible. She had suddenly been left with the task of raising all five children alone, a fate she clearly resented. The past years had not been kind to her and she buried her frustrations inside, causing her to turn bitter and angry. Her mouth, once lit with smiles so warm and friendly, now had become drawn tightly into a straight, thin line. Her lilting gospel tunes ceased to fill the house long ago, along with any maternal encouragement or words of motherly praise to her children.

Things could have been worse, I told myself as I neared the elegantly cut and nicely painted white front steps leading into the house. I mean, I could be destitute and moving to an even worse looking place than we had just left and be all alone in this situation, without a friend or ally. At least John, Raa, and my brother David still stood staunchly by my side.

Actually, I don't know what I would have done without their support. I was a big girl now, felt almost like a woman, and I could not stand on my own two feet as well as the next person. Without John's love and gentle direction, Raa's strength, and my brother David's happy-go-lucky attitude, it would have almost been unbearable.

The porch floorboards, lacquered to a high white luster, felt sturdy beneath my feet as I neared the open doorway. The large windows which flanked the doorway were clear and clean and through them I could see the draperies which had been drawn against the unrelentless summer sun. The fabric of these draperies was of a heavy and rich pastel colored material, elegant and understated. Interested to finally see what surprises might lie in wait for me inside the house, I walked through the open front door.

Like walking into a wall, the musty smell of a hundred years hit me with its full force as soon as I stepped into the living room. Voices, it seemed of a thousand people, pelted my ears. Some wept, some screamed and others shouted various obscenities in guttural tones.

The room was littered with endless bodies, all bleeding and wounded, dying or past human help. Human figures scurried from one bloodied body to the next, tending wounds of the living or closing the eyes of the dead. The smell of blood was so thick, I could taste its saltiness on my tongue. In seconds I became aware of other odors, those of gunpowder, morphine and chloroform. The atmosphere was suffocating and soon I found it hard to even breathe. A man from across the room began to scream and hold onto his crushed and mangled leg. Another man, dressed in a long overcoat, approached him, holding a hand saw. The man, still scream-ing, struggled against two women who were trying to hold him down in bed, thwarting the attempts of two other women who unsuccessfully tried to place a wet rag over his nose and mouth.

By this time the man in the long overcoat was standing

over him. Words were exchanged between the two men I couldn't decipher. The man with the bad leg seemed to be pleading but the man with the hand saw didn't seem to listen. Instead, he positioned the blade above the man's knee. The man began to scream again just before he fainted from the pain.

"Carol! Carol!" my mother shouted to me, breaking the spell under which I had fallen. "Help us uncover this furniture."

"Yes, Mama," I replied, shaking my head to clear my vision as I focused on the room in which I stood, stepping back once more into the present reality.

If what I had just seen and experienced had shocked me, the beauty of the living room I stood in left me pleasantly surprised. The interior, like the outside of the house, was of a classical design. The ceilings were high and the borders were trimmed lovingly with delicate gingerbread mouldings. Every wall and ceiling had been painted white, reflecting the freshness of the exterior. The floors were made of polished hardwood and shined with a high lacquered glow. Throw rugs fashioned with intricate designs, though a little worn in places, looked as if they had been imported from some far away and mysterious land. I was soon, apart from my recent experience, falling in love with our new home.

Pulling the drop cloths off the living room furniture was almost better than Christmas. Between shouts of excitement and gasps of delight we managed to rid the furniture of their shrouds within a few short minutes. Overstuffed sofas and chairs graced the room. Tables of the finest cherrywood had been arranged strategically near the sofas and chairs, showing to the best advantage their beauty and splendor. Our most exquisite find was a large antique china cabinet whose interior was stocked with the prettiest china plates, cups and saucers I had ever seen. The pieces were so delicate that you could almost see through the soft milkiness of the porcelain, your vision only obscured by the tiny pattern of pink rosebuds. Looking around at the splendor of the room, I felt as though I were in some sort of fantastic fairytale. I instinctively pinched myself to make sure I hadn't tripped into some other dimension.

I looked at my mother who was standing in the middle of the room, overcome with as much awe as myself. For the first time in days I saw a hint of a smile reach her lips as she appraised her surroundings and something fleeting like the glow of appreciation or happiness warmed her eyes. But then the expression was soon erased, leaving only a cool indifference in its wake.

"I see we have much to do before it gets dark," my mother said, looking at each one of us in turn. "Boys you start unpacking the truck," she ordered, "and Carol, you can help me put things away."

"Yes, Mama," we all replied obediently without so much as a hesitation.

The home, as big and beautiful as it was, was like moving to a place of yesteryear, a step backward in time. No running water or indoor plumbing was evident and instead of tractors to plow the massive fields, we had two work horses we named Pet and Mail.

For two days we worked, only taking time to fall into an exhausted sleep or eat a cold and quick meal. By the end of the second day, completely stretched to our physical limits and ready to drop where we stood, we could see that we were finally finished. We had pushed ourselves even harder when we discovered that as the unpacking progressed and the house began to take shape, our mother's attitude began to soften. We all understood that purchasing this home represented a fresh start for her. She had sold our old farm, so many miles away, along with all of her painful memories of hardship and loneliness. Strangely though, as my mother's heart began to lighten, mine began to sink.

Ever since I had first walked into the house I had felt, along with joyful surprise, an overwhelming sense of sadness and try as I might, I found I couldn't quite shake the memory of what I had seen. The screams and pain of the hysterical amputee had already begun to haunt my dreams. Last night I had woke lathered in perspiration, as I felt the two women holding me down as the man in the overcoat began to cut into my leg. Luckily, I hadn't shouted or awakened my family. Far from being understanding, they were always quick to ridicule, stemming more from ignorance and fear than anything else. An incident involving Raa which had taken place during the move hadn't helped matters any, but it made me smile with secret satisfaction nonetheless. Since there was only room in the cab of our truck to comfortably seat two people, they being my mother and uncle, the rest of us were required to ride in the back with the furniture and household items. In order to make it to our destination in one trip, my uncle had enclosed one of his trucks to hold everything — including all of us kids. He fashioned a wooden structure covering the exposed truck bed. This wooden shell made it impossible to see out into the surrounding countryside as we drove along the highway. Well, it didn't take long for Ricky to find a place in the wooden shell where a knothole at eye level had conveniently come loose and fallen out, making a perfect porthole to the outside world. Time after time, I tried to take a turn looking out the eye hole, but each and every time, being the only girl, I was pushed aside by my brothers. After two days of this treatment, the weather as hot as everyone's tempers, I became a little more than angry and demanded to have my turn. Raa, who sat patiently next to me throughout the entire ordeal, was growing more restless by the minute. I finally confronted Ricky who sat planted in front of the coveted window. I decided it was time to push him away from the hole. He met my feeble effort with a shove that sent me flying across the truck bed, over an upside down table and chair and into the side of the wooden inclosure. With a thunderous sound, I hit my head. After this action, Raa had finally had enough of my brother's bullied roughhousing. With a deafening roar, all eyes turning in fear toward the big cat, Raa leaped from where he had been resting across the truck bed and landed directly in front of my brother Ricky. Not until this moment had anyone, but myself, seen Raa. Eyes wide, big as saucers, my brother Ricky was the first to react. He jumped away from the tiger, toward the front of the truck bed, to the cab, falling backward in the process. Scrambling to his feet he reached the cab, all the while screaming and pounding on it, trying to alert my mother and uncle to stop the truck. My other brothers, sitting in the truck with me, had already began to shout as soon as Raa had appeared. By the time Ricky had reached the cab, the situation inside the wooden shell had turned into an all out pandemonium. I watched as a blur of male bodies pushed and shoved their way over and across the furniture and household boxes to the rear of the truck. It was a wonder with all that weight and pounding that the truck didn't fall apart.

During the melee, satisfied with his protective measure, Raa crossed casually to where I sat and laid down comfortably at my feet, where he began with his paw a normal feline ritual of grooming. Though he seemed completely involved with what he was doing, I noticed he continued watching my brothers and did so until the truck finally came to an abrupt halt, throwing my brothers standing in the rear off balance and onto the floor of the truck bed. I knew I shouldn't have, but I began to laugh, drawing all eyes accusingly toward me. But their stares lasted for only a few moments. Everyone was so excited to tell their rendition of the attack to my mother while yelling "large cat!" that they had forgotten to pay much attention to me. The story that finally met with everyone's approval was wilder than any I could have told. They all agreed that some wild cat, though no one could agree on what kind of cat, had just appeared out of nowhere, and attacked them. Of course, I was accused with being the mad person involved with the cat and the attack. I could tell by the way my mother and uncle were shaking their heads that they didn't believe a word of what was told to them.

When asked to tell my version of the cat story, I simply stated that I had seen my friend Raa. My reply didn't go over very well to say the least, but amid the scoffing and contemptible glares, I knew they remembered my stories of Raa. Thereafter, though I was not treated with overly kindness, I was suddenly tolerated and when it was my turn to look through the crude window of the truck on our remaining journey, I was allowed to do so without any interference. My brothers had viewed me warily before Raa's sudden appearance but had at least spoken to me and considered me as, if not one of the boys, at least one of the family. Somehow since Raa's manifestation the break between my family and myself had become wider, causing me to feel alienated and alone.

John, who I relied on for support and friendship, had even seemed to desert me. He had been absent the entire duration of our trip and hadn't even checked in since our arrival. At least Raa had remained at my side, my constant companion and reliable friend.

I tried to go back to sleep, but it proved useless. Besides feeling the lingering shock of my nightmare, I was thirsty and hot. I decided, without much ado, to go into the kitchen for a glass of cool, well water I had brought in earlier. I knew the water would quench my thirst and sober my thoughts enough to help me go back to sleep. But while I made my way down the stairs to the kitchen, I had the uneasy feeling I was being watched. Once or twice I thought I caught the figure of someone or something out of the corner of my eye. At first I shrugged it off as nothing, merely a shadow or misplaced moonbeam. Perhaps a piece of furniture that was out of place or a discarded article of clothing. But as I reached the kitchen I knew it was something more, something real. I could feel its strong life-force energy. I turned to face my unseen companion, but only shadows and stilled darkness greeted me. It hadn't occurred to me before, but I suddenly realized it might be my brother Ricky. Always the prankster, he loved to sneak up from behind and try to scare me. It had been a long standing game between us since we were small children. It frustrated him to no end because I could feel his presence yards away and would always catch him before he was able to strike.

With a wry smile, ready to call his hand once again, I centered my energy as John had taught me years ago. I felt the familiar warmth begin to generate in my solar plexus chakra. As I felt the yellow heat move and quicken in a circular motion, I began to push the energy outward from my body to the figure watching me from the darkness of the hallway. Within moments we were connected. I knew right away that it wasn't my brother. I began to panic and as I did a shot of energy as powerful as any lightening bolt shot through my body, shoving me backwards and onto the floor with its force. The electric current running through my body was so acute that I sat paralyzed, frozen to the floor where I sat. The mixed feelings of sadness, anger and grief consumed my soul. I tried to pull my energy away from the source of my torment, but the more I tried to pull away, the stronger the tug came from the other end. My energy had become tapped at my solar plexus and was quickly being sucked dry. As I grew weaker, the life-force I was battling grew stronger. My fear, overpowering me and growing by the second, only added to my adversary's strength. I tried to scream, feeling it well in my throat, but the sound wouldn't come. Like my body, my voice had become imprisoned by the energy vampire who seemed determined to bleed me of my very essence.

From where I sat, I saw the entity begin to manifest, starting to take shape at the end of the golden cord to which I was helplessly connected. All at once, like a flower bursting from a bud, it took shape. I tried to scream again, but remained paralyzed staring in mute horror at the apparition which stood before me.

The face I recognized immediately. It was the face that I had focused on in my nightmare and vision. Though he was standing on two legs, I knew I sat facing the young amputee soldier. His clothes, which consisted of a grey confederate uniform and worn, black boots, were battlestained and bloodied. His sabre, the blade notched by countless battles hung heavily at his side, proudly bearing, at the hilt, tassels of red and yellow. He began to advance toward me and my fear returned, overriding my present curiosity.

With every essence of my being, I called out for John, my teacher. Unable to verbalize my desperate plea, I shouted his name mentally, until I felt my head was ready to explode.

In an instant, a blue ball of energy materialized between the soldier and myself. I heard John's voice clearly in my head, calm and gentle.

"Relax, Carol," John instructed. "Let go of the fear. Release it, let it go."

My fear, with the reassurance of John's presence, quickly receded. As soon as I relaxed, the cord connecting me to the entity dissolved. Able to move for the first time in what seemed hours, I slumped over into an exhausted huddle.

"Look at him, Carol," John coaxed, now fully materializing at my side.

It took all my remaining strength to do what he asked. I had no great desire to look back at my recent and still visible nightmare.

"Relax and look," John stated firmly, obviously not willing to take no for an answer.

Reluctantly, I raised my eyes to the entity across the room. With any fear I had previously felt gone, I was able to clearly look at the young soldier. My heart went out to him immediately. His eyes contained a heavy sadness, filled with an intense grief and pain. Tears spilled over his lashes and down his proud, well-defined cheekbones, falling and dampening the grey fabric of his dirty uniform. His shoulders sagged and heaved in silent sobs as I continued to watch.

"How could I have possibly been afraid of him?" I asked, my heart breaking with his grief.

"You were just taken unaware and weren't prepared for your meeting," John explained simply. "You created a monster out of your fear. This poor soul has been caught between the two worlds. He is not alive in the physical sense, nor does he realize he has died on a spiritual level. This displaced soul is in constant pain and turmoil, knowing he must go somewhere to escape his confusing and painful environment, but unsure as to where or how to move on.

"He felt the energy you put out and attached himself to you, hungry, actually starving to connect with another life-force. He was compelled by his own ancient soul memory to go toward the light, and your energy was so intense he instinctively was attracted to you. Your energy acts like a beacon with these spirits, drawing them to you like moths to a flame. This is an important lesson because once you can overcome your fear, you can help to guide these souls into the next dimension where they belong, to the greatest light of all, the light of universal love."

As I listened to John, I couldn't help watching the grieving soldier. It was hard for me to believe that only moments before, this handsome young man was the center of my fear.

"John," I asked when he had finished, "why did the figure first appear to me as some nightmarish figure, when in fact it was something entirely different?"

"What next to love is the most powerful emotion?" John asked.

"Fear," I replied, trying to recall my former lessons.

"Exactly," he replied, obviously pleased with my adept answer. "Fear is a powerful emotion. The more powerful the emotion, the more intense the energy. Love usually grows slowly and holds fast, but fear is instant. The more you feared the despairing soul, the more frightening it became to you. He played off your fear. This is the way of hauntings. When you connected with the entity it held on to your energy source and felt your fear, or most powerful emotion. Fear leaves you spiritually unprotected and vulnerable, enabling the entity to pull your energy away from you and into itself. On first sight you saw the figure through eyes that had been clouded by fear, now you see this soul with the clear vision of love and understanding. Only by seeing the apparition in this light can you become free of your fear. Actually, it's a good thing you are no longer afraid. He's not the only one trapped here. I can feel and see many more. We'll start by helping this one over to the next dimension right now and hopefully in the next few days we'll be able to get to the rest of them.

"Close your eyes, Carol," John stated, aware of my dilemma. "Pull your energy into your heart center and become still within yourself. Don't allow the fear to over take you. Relax. Be quiet and still. Take a deep breath and settle your emotions. Nothing is going to scare you as long as you are centered. Just relax."

I could hear the soldier as he continued his pitiful sobbing, obviously still caught in the throngs of his own nightmare.

"I want you to balance yourself by pulling all of your energy into your heart center," John stated as he placed his hand, palm facing toward me, a few inches away from my chest.

I could feel the heat of his energy penetrating my heart center. As I concentrated on this one spot, I began to feel my energy rush from my limbs, up through my torso, and down through my head to my heart area. All of my being was suddenly concentrated in this one particular area. It was a tranquil and peaceful warmth I was feeling. I could feel my physical body blending in perfect harmony with my higher self and had easily moved into this higher state of consciousness.

"Well, I guess I must be a good teacher," he said in thought. "You did what you were supposed to do before I had a chance to tell you!"

The world I had become a part of, I noticed as John was speaking, was filled with vibrant color and light. John's body emitted beautiful hues of the purest blue, turning his already blue robe into a resplendent garment of pulsating blue light. I stood hypnotized by the beauty of his spiritual body.

"Never mind me, Carol," John replied, responding to my stare. "Look at the one behind you who needs your help."

With that thought in mind, without having to turn, I stood before the grieving man.

Strangely enough, unlike John, he seemed covered in a dark cloud, imprisoned in a thousand strands of dark colors, which wrapped around him like heavy cobwebs.

Caught in his own inner turmoil, he seemed oblivious to John and me. Only once or twice did he look in our direction, as if he were looking for someone or something in particular, but he soon stopped his searching and returned to his eternal sorrow.

"Look at the cloud which hangs over him, Carol," John stated, standing and walking, actually hovering, to where I stood. "He is cloaked in a dark web of confusion and fear. He is so tangled in his own state of turmoil, that the light of understanding and love can't penetrate the walls of which he is held prisoner. In the physical form it's not much different. People allow their fear and confusion to trap them in the same web, a web they are unable to escape. In body or out, it is always the same when dealing with fear or confusion.

"The entity knows we're here. He can feel our warmth and the presence of love and understanding. He just doesn't know how to come near it. This adds to his perpetual confusion and allows the strands of fear to tighten even more closely around him, completely obscuring his ability to join with the universal consciousness of which we are all a part.

"Your energy when you connected with him, was so strong that it penetrated his wall of chaos. He held onto your light and energy as a thirsty man would water. He had been encased in his own darkness for so long that your light was a beacon of hope to a lost traveler. The light at the end of a long road, so to speak. It is now time for you to connect with him, not in fear as you did before, but with love and understanding. It is time to break the chains of fear which bind around him and send him on his way."

"How can we do that?" I asked wanting more than anything to end the pain of this grieving soul.

"You have already begun," John replied. "Just send the love you feel out toward him and watch."

As I looked at the man I felt my love begin to grow. Every inch, every part of my being, became filled with the warmth and beauty of pure and unconditional love. I became a universal channel of love and I reveled in the heady feeling. A sweet, rapturous euphoria spread throughout my being until I thought I would burst with it. Music, so splendid and filled with a thousand heavenly voices, penetrated each particle of my spiritual essence. I had never known such all-consuming ecstasy, such complete balance and satisfaction. Like a magnificent tidal wave it poured through me as I pushed the energy out to where the grieving man stood, covering him in a wondrous blanket of pinkish-white light. Slowly, one by one, as the rosy light wrapped around his figure, the heavy dark threads of fear which bound him gradually melted away into nothingness.

When the last cloud of darkness vanished, and the loving waves of energy running through me had stabilized into a gentle, peaceful lull, he looked at us as if awakening from a deep unrestful sleep.

"How long have I been here?" he asked quietly, the glow of universal love encasing him in an aura of pinkish-white light.

"Long enough," John replied, walking to where he

stood, taking the man's hand in his own.

"Where am I and where have I been?" the soldier questioned, looking at John, his eyes calm and full of acceptance.

"You have been between the worlds, my brother, but now it is time for us to lead you home," John replied comfortingly. "Come and walk with us."

With John's words, we were standing, or hovering, in front of an area filled with an intense, bright golden light. I recognized the place immediately. This was the place I had last seen my father. There were no doors, no ceilings, or floors. No physical construction of any kind, just tranquil endless space. I felt instinctively pulled to the light and longed to cross over into the next dimension with this kindred spirit, but the tug of the physical world was still too strong and it kept me securely anchored in the realm of which I was still a part.

The man looked at us for a moment before advancing toward the light. His eyes were filled with boundless joy and happiness. Words were unnecessary to convey his feelings.

"Go and grow in love and wisdom," John said, giving the man a warm embrace.

The man just smiled and shook his head in acknowledgement and turned toward the light. Within moments after crossing the brilliant threshold, he was gone from sight. I wasn't sure but it seemed I heard his voice from far away, thanking us for what we had done.

"Let's go back now, Carol," John said, taking my hand in his.

In a flash we were once again standing in the middle of my kitchen.

"That was wonderful," I sighed, still enjoying the effects of our experience.

"It always is," John replied, adjusting the folds of his white robe, he had changed his apparel somehow between dimensions. "But more importantly, it was just as wonderful an experience for our misguided brother as it was for you. Always remember universal love consciousness works both ways. When you give, you can't help but receive it back. This is the way of the universe. As you give, so shall you receive, or, as you sow, so shall you reap. I can't say it anymore succinctly than that. It's time for you to sleep now, Carol. We have much to do tomorrow and I need my favorite student wide awake and fully aware for her lessons." With that bit of advice, John was gone.

I drifted back to my bedroom on what seemed a cloud of joy, where dreams, once I tucked myself into my soft bed, came easily.

I awoke with the strange sensation of being lightly poked or tapped on my shoulder. Discounting it, I pulled the bed covers, in my half-conscious state, up over my shoulder to my ear, hoping to catch a few more winks of sleep. This was the wrong thing to do. As soon as I pulled up the covers, someone yanked them down, completely exposing my night-gown-clad body. Why that angry someone was trying to wake me so early in the morning, I did not know, but I sat upright in bed, ready to catch the irritating prankster. The only problem was that there wasn't any. It didn't take me very long to put two and two together. Math was never one of my strongest subjects, but in this case two and two equaled ghosts.

Forgetting everything John had taught me the night before, I ran out of my bedroom as fast as my legs would carry me and down the stairs to the kitchen where I knew my mother was fixing breakfast, all the while screaming "ghost!" at the top of my voice, fear once again being my primary motivator.

I heard the sound of a plate crash from the kitchen as I neared the doorway. When I arrived breathless at my destination, the scene of spilled oatmeal, a broken dish and a glaring mother greeted me.

"What's the matter with you, Carol?" my mother shouted,

squatting to wipe up the sticky gruel covering the kitchen floor. "You scared me half to death. Your shouting is enough to wake the dead!"

"That's what I mean!" I stammered. "The dead are awake, I mean, the ghosts are here. I mean, I saw a ghost. No, I didn't see it exactly, but I felt it."

"You were dreaming again," my mother responded sternly, cleaning up the last pieces of the shattered china and our ruined breakfast.

By this time, my brothers, awakened by my tirade, had gradually all assembled into the kitchen for an explanation. By the looks on their faces they were obviously not impressed with my wild reasonings.

One shook his head, another one snorted and rolled his eyes up to the ceiling, while another rotated his finger near his head in a circular motion, indicating that I was crazy. Only David looked at me with concern, his eyes full of compassion and understanding.

"I wasn't dreaming!" I pleaded, adamantly refusing to acquiesce. "There are ghosts in the house."

"Right, and I'm the president of the United States!" my brother Mark interjected, causing everyone in the room to howl with laughter.

That is, everyone but my brother David and my mother.

"Boys, quiet!" my mother snapped, causing a quick silence to fall over the room. "And as for you, young lady, I don't ever want to hear about ghosts again. That includes auras, dying, or pet tigers named Raa. I've had just about enough from you and I mean it! Do you understand?"

"But Mama," I started in protest, but looking at my mother's unyielding countenance, I knew that any other arguing was futile. "Yes, Mama," I answered meekly, ignoring my brothers snickering.

"Good," my mother stated firmly. "Now, get dressed, you have chores to do," she said, then turned toward the kitchen doorway where my brothers stood. "And that means all of you!" she scolded, sending my brothers scampering down the hallway to their rooms.

I knew any further discussion of the incident would be useless. Actually, I shouldn't have mentioned ghosts in the first place. I had learned that bit of information a long time ago. The whole incident this morning was my own fault. I had let my fear get the best of me, and until I could learn to harness it, it would most certainly continue to get the best of me.

I quickly dressed and made my bed, this time without any ghostly interference, and walked down the stairs to the kitchen. When I entered the room, I noticed my brothers and mother were already seated and well into eating their fare of breakfast, and the laughter I had heard while walking toward the kitchen had stopped abruptly as soon as I appeared.

The uncomfortable silence prevailed as I took my seat at the table. All of my brothers were smiling with inner amusement as they ate, unwilling to look up at me and lose their fragile composure. Only my mother remained unamused, instead she seemed completely unattached, lost in some private far away thought.

To them it was a dream. To me, reality. And since the reality was mine, I was the one who had to deal with it and deal with it I would. The fear was my problem, clear and simple. The monster was my own and I knew, not John, not Raa, or anyone else could conquer it for me. I looked down at the bowl of oatmeal sitting in front of me on the table. It had been some time since it had been placed there, waiting to be eaten. Now, cold and stiff, it was anything but appetizing. I picked up my spoon and raised it with a half-hearted effort above the bowl, ready to attempt at least a bite of the cold mixture. As I did so, I heard another whisper and a snicker from down the table. I turned, glaring toward the originator of the noise. The culprit, Peter, chose instead to ignore me and continued attacking the last remaining pieces of oatmeal sticking to the rim of his bowl, scraping the sides of the glass container irritatingly as he did so. Any appetite I might have had was soon gone, along with any table manners Peter might have once possessed. I placed my spoon back down on the table next to the bowl of uneaten gruel. I politely excused myself from the company of my family, leaving without doing the dishes, since today it was my brother David's turn, and settled into doing my chores.

As I walked up to the front door, having finished my chores, I mulled over my experiences of the last day and evening. Having come to grips with my problem, I felt quite confident I had finally overcome my sense of fear. My confidence was short lived.

The front screen, when I reached for it, was suddenly oozing with a red, sticky substance that could only be blood. So much for confidence. My reaction time was so quick that I stumbled down the front porch steps in my haste to get away from the door.

I ran past the chicken house, raced by the old sawmill and far up into the foothills behind my house. I ran until my legs were unwilling to carry me any further, my body wet and drenched with perspiration.

I sought out the solace of a nearby pine and sat at its base, enjoying the soothing protection of its shade. I was so exhausted, I felt as if I wanted to cry, but the tears wouldn't come. Instead, I stared down at our distant house, a fresh reminder of my fear and self-disappointment.

"It's not easy, is it?" I heard John ask as he materialized and sat next to me, leaning his back against the trunk of the mighty pine.

"I don't want to go back there," I replied somberly, completely ignoring John's question, hoping my friend was willing to support my unreasonable decision.

"Why not?" he asked as soon as I had finished the sentence, obviously not ready to agree with my rash decision.

"Because of what's happening," I replied. I was ready to drop the entire subject.

I had realized a little too late that John wasn't going to give me any friendly comfort. I picked up a pine cone and began to examine it in my hand, giving John a clear indication the discussion was closed.

"I see," he replied with a tolerant sigh, then continued as he watched what I was doing. "It's a nice pine cone, Carol, but it's not going to help you with what you have to do. You can't refuse to acknowledge your fear. Now instead of just being afraid of things that disturb you, you are now afraid of being afraid. It's not going to get any better you know, it's just going to gradually get worse. You thought the screen trick unnerved you, just continue to ignore your fear and then see what will happen."

"I thought I learned how to face my fear last night?" I replied in exasperation, turning toward John as I dropped the forgotten pine cone to the ground.

"You did," he responded, "but not completely or what you have been experiencing wouldn't be happening right now."

"Why didn't you tell me these things were going to happen?" I said accusingly. "Why didn't you let me know?"

"You had to experience it for yourself," he replied. "Experience is the best teacher. Working through this experience will give you tools which you can carry with you to use later on in life. Words come and go, but the experience is yours forever.

"This tree will help to ground you as we work through our meditation. Feel yourself become one with the tree. Follow in your mind's eye the path of its roots probing deep within the earth. Follow the path and become one with the tree. Follow the path and become, with every foot downward, more anchored as you penetrate deeper into the heart of the earth."

Without much prompting I began to feel the roots growing and pushing downward through the soft dirt. Soon I was one with the tree feeling solid and well grounded.

I could hear John's voice inside my head helping me, and I could feel his energy tying me into the roots of the tree.

"Now, Carol, let's pull a spirit from the house to work with. I'll help you to free this person from their pain," John spoke in a calm, strong voice.

Soon I saw a soldier in front of me, dressed in his fatigues, looking afraid and so tired.

I asked for his highest spirit guides to come in and help give him insight so this entity could see the light. And as I did this, two beings appeared beside the soldier and gently took his hands. The guides, John and myself walked him toward a beautiful golden light.

When we arrived at the light and proceeded to walk into it, I felt the love that seemed to vibrate through my body. It ran through my body like soft electricity, warming and vibrating every nerve, every muscle, every cell in my being. I looked at the soldier and knew that he was feeling the same love that I was. It was so wonderful! I wanted to stay there and bask in this light and love forever.

Then I heard John's voice and something pulled me. Once again, I felt the rough trunk of the pine tree against me. I was back.

I opened my eyes to see John's look. It was a pure, straightforward, honest gaze that said kindness even before he spoke. "Now, I'd like to go back with you to your house, and help you to conquer your fear. We'll clean out that house so you can live in your own home peacefully."

With those words, he placed his hand in mine, and pulled me to my feet. We began the walk down the hill to the house in comfortable silence.

After a quick dinner, I rushed through the dishes as fast as I possibly could so I could escape to the solace of my room. Once there, I slipped into my nightgown and snuggled under the covers. Soon I felt a definite presence. I could sense that the presence was not John or Raa, yet I knew

John's strength was with me. I inhaled deeply and closed my eyes. In my mind's eye I saw a soul standing at the foot of my bed with a hand outstretched, gesturing for help. Suddenly, I felt energy surge up and flow through me. Right then, I asked for his highest guides to come and help us. Two very subtle, but steady lights lit up beside him, and a beautiful woman took hold of his hand and gently led him toward the shaft of golden light.

I felt a surge of love and confidence flow through me as the soul moved to the place he belonged, that place of love existing in the golden light. Right at the moment I let go and felt his complete release, I opened my eyes to see my mother standing in my doorway, the hall light illuminating her shadow so she appeared ominous and towering above me. I felt rather than saw, her glare, piercing eyes bore into mine. I knew the feeling well, I didn't need any light to tell me what it meant. I lowered my gaze from hers and kept quiet, afraid to even breathe.

"Carol, what on earth are you up to?" her flat, even voice penetrated the silence.

"Nothing, Mama," was all I could muster for a reply. And a whispered reply at that.

"Don't tell me nothing, young lady," she started in that same quiet, flat voice, "I have eyes, I can see. You didn't even look like yourself when I came in here." Her voice rose with each word, "Your up to no good again, I can tell, and you better stop this nonsense if you know what's good for you!"

I cowed under her menacing glare and shouting words.

"Yes, Mama," was all I could push out. I slowly brought the covers up to my chin, never taking my eyes off my mother.

She slammed the door shut like a final word and I heard her steps echo in the hall as she stomped down the stairs.

I curled down under the covers, pulling them completely over my head. No way, I thought defiantly, no way would I stop what I enjoyed most. Cleaning out this house was necessary if we were all going to live in it happily. How could I just stop helping those poor souls? I once again conjured up the love inside me from the golden light and I let go of the feeling of my mother's wrath and lulled gently into a dreamless sleep.

Morning arrived quickly, making it seem as though I had just closed my eyes, not yet the time to awaken. But it was morning and my chores awaited me. Before scrambling into my clothes, I took a moment to look back into the night to see if I had dreamt, but I saw nothing, just black sleep.

Excitement permeated the air and as a result, I moved much quicker and lighter than usual in the early morning chill. As I bounded down the stairs, releasing even more excited energy, a form suddenly loomed up in front of me. Its presence stopped me dead in my tracks, I was so surprised. Then I steadied myself by taking a deep breath and asking John for his help inside my mind. An electrified jolt of energy shot through me, almost knocking me off-balance. As I steadied myself, I realized this energy was from John, although he was no where to be seen. I took another large breath and started to talk to the shadowed form not more than two feet in front of me.

"Do you need help?" I asked from within me. The form hovered closer to me, not responding. I stood my ground. "Okay, look for the shaft of golden light," I said as I pictured in my mind a golden stream of light just to the left of him. I watched as he was being drawn into that direction, and soon he was completely aglow with the light, drenched in golden flecks of light particles. Again I felt a surge of energy run through me, and that same feeling of release I experienced the night before. Once again I felt so light and happy. I continued my excited descent down the stairs, when I came face to face with Mama and Ricky. It was clearly evident by their expressions that they had witnessed the whole scene. Expecting another blow up from Mama, she just shook her head in disbelief and retreated to the kitchen, Ricky following close at her heels, imitating her shaking head.

I felt safer being outside, away from their mocking stares, and I took my time completing my chores, milking Betsy and feeding the chickens.

When I returned from the barn, I entered the kitchen to find Mama sitting at the table, sipping a cup of aromatic black coffee. The silence and the steam from the coffee were the only things that hung in the air. Without warning, she suddenly spoke.

"Carol, come here, honey," she said in a quiet, soft voice, nothing like her tone yesterday. She gestured for me to sit down, and I did so quietly. She lifted the cup to take another sip of coffee, then lowered it again, as if what she was about to say was too important to interrupt with coffee. "Honey, what's going on?" she said, still in a soft voice. I tried not to let that soft voice get to me. I saw streaks of color in her aura and a feeling came through. I couldn't put my finger on the exact feeling, but it was a familiar feeling, one I had felt before. What was she up to? I didn't answer her, my silence prompted her more.

"Carol, now you can tell me, can't you?" she wheedled. "I won't tell anyone. It can be our secret. You know I love you, honey. I wouldn't ever hurt you." She was staring at me like she was my best friend, not my mother.

"N . . . nothing, Mama," I stammered, finally finding my voice.

She just shook her head like I was a lost cause or something. Then she turned her attention back to her cup of coffee, as if it were the most important cup of coffee in the world. I took advantage of her lack of attention to slip out of the kitchen quietly.

I wandered into the living room where I picked up a book and started turning the pages, looking at the pictures. Not long after that, Mama came into the room and began dusting off the tables singing the chorus of "You are my

Sunshine" in an overly happy voice. Halfway through the next verse and two tables later, she turned to me and smiled.

"Carol, you know you are my little sunshine," she said, "and I want to understand what's happening with you so that I can help you."

I looked at her, all traces of disbelief vanished from my mind. She wanted to understand me! She wanted to love me and understand and help me! I wanted her to understand, and more than anything, I wanted my mama to love me. My emotional part was brimming with love and it overflowed into my intuition, clouding and confusing that side of me. In a jumbled moment of enthusiasm and love, I burst forth with my thoughts.

"Oh, Mama," I said breathlessly, "I'm helping people who have died in this old house many years ago during the civil war. They don't know they have died and they're stuck here, so I'm helping them to move on to a place where they belong." In my rushed explanation, I failed to notice Mama's features grow dark. She stood there, that mean glare replaced her fake smile. Oh God, I can't believe I said that to her, I thought much too late.

"I knew you were up to something of the devil," she spoke, a storm brewing in her tone. "I just knew it! You have to stop this right now. How come you're like this?" she was speaking more to herself now, chastising herself for the wicked child she believed she had. "I don't deserve a child like you!" she screamed louder and louder, her hands holding my shoulders and shaking as if she could shake it out of me. She kept shaking and screaming, "I've got to get that devil out of you!" She was shaking me so hard, my teeth rattled.

David came running into the house, yelling, "What's wrong? What's wrong?"

Mama quit shaking me and turned toward David, her face a deep shade of red. "Carol's crazy, she's just crazy!" and with those words she stormed off in the direction of the kitchen, yelling to herself, "That child is full of the devil. What am I to do . . ."

David turned me toward him, tears burned my eyes and my body shook by itself now, frightened by the whole ordeal.

"She's just upset, Carol," David said in a low voice. "I'm sure she didn't mean all those things she said. What did you do to set her off?"

I just shook my head, indicating I didn't want to talk about it, and ran straight up to my room, locking the door behind me, crying myself into sleep. Exhausted, I slept the rest of the day and all through the night.

Morning came and I dreaded getting up and going downstairs. The memory of yesterday came flooding back to me as I sat in my bed, unwilling to move toward the bustling day. Finally, with a sheer force of will, I pushed myself to get dressed and crept downstairs. To my surprise, I heard the familiar laughter and joking of the boys coming from the back porch. I sighed an invisible sigh of relief, everything was back to normal. Or so I naively thought. When I entered the kitchen, there stood Mama, a black cloud hung around her head like a huge thunderstorm cloud, ready to burst. I knew that meant she was depressed, I could tell that by just looking at her face.

"Carol, we're going into town today, shopping, for food," she said, in a clipped manner. "So clean yourself up. I told Peter to do your chores today." Then she resumed her preparations of lunch for the boys since we wouldn't be home that afternoon.

I dared not question her in the fragile position I was in, so I went about cleaning myself up. I poured some of the hot water from the pot on the wood stove into a shallow tin pan and drew a bucket of cold water from the well on the back porch to even out the temperature. I tried to be quick about the cleaning, but the tepid water felt so good, so warm and comforting, that I lingered just a little in its watery embrace.

When finally the water grew cool, I finished in the kitchen and hurriedly went upstairs to put on a clean dress.

I didn't feel at all right about this shopping day. For one thing, Ricky or Peter always went with Mama to town for large quantities of food, never me. Secondly, we had a country store only two miles away that we used for little pick ups, and by the look of the pantry, we didn't need more than a bag of cornmeal and maybe some sugar. What was going on here?

That question kept turning over in my mind as my mother and I rode in silence all the way into town. I kept my gaze focused outside the car's window, mesmerized by the farms and houses, and people working in the fields. I specifically did not look at my mother once. I knew she was up to something and with a jolt, I realized what that feeling was. The feeling I couldn't pinpoint yesterday was that of distrust. I felt it now, loud and clear. The hurt and betrayal stung like a thousand wasps, and I vowed not to let trust cloud my emotions again.

Gradually the houses started appearing closer and closer together and the view became that of a busy town. We drove right past the big market without even slowing down. I watched the building until it was completely out of sight. My mother didn't say a word.

Where are we going? I asked myself silently, definitely not to get food. A picture of our church sprang up in my mind. Sure enough, we made a turn onto another street and soon we arrived at our church.

Mama looked long and hard at me before she spoke.

"Well, young lady, here we are. Let's see what a man of God has to say to someone like you."

Before we even had a chance to get out of the car, Brother Thomas came out to greet us.

"Jewell, so good to see you," he said warmly in greeting. His smile stretched from ear to ear. His smile subdued when he looked into my mother's eyes. "Come, let's go to my office." And he took my mother's hand, the two of them walking ahead of me while I trailed warily behind.

The church seemed to echo every minute movement as we walked through its wooden expanse to the tiny room in the back, Brother Thomas' office. He indicated to two chairs on the other side of his desk, gesturing for us to sit. Then he closed the heavy door, and for a moment, I felt like a prisoner who had just had the jail door unfairly slammed and locked on him. I shuddered at the thought of this being like a prison.

"Well, Jewell, what can I do for you?" he began quietly. Although he was speaking to Mama, he looked right at me.

Mama burst forth with wild accusations, talking so fast it was almost like a blur. The words and sentence ran over one another and I could barely catch a word of it. Words like "devil" and "evil" and "nonsense" once again filled her vocabulary, and what she was saying, although I'd heard it many a time before, sounded even more harsh and accusing than ever. What she was saying shocked me so much, I felt frozen to my chair.

Then I heard her tell Brother Thomas what I had told her yesterday, what I had *confided* to her, what she had sworn would be "our little secret". How could she do this to me? Instead of just feeling frozen, all of a sudden I felt like someone had smashed me into a thousand tiny icy shards. I felt shattered. And that same awful feeling of betrayal surrounded me.

When Mama was finished, Brother Thomas turned to me. "Carol, do you know about hell?" he asked, not one bit of warmth left in his features. He continued, and it was a good thing he didn't wait for an answer, because I could've given him one that would've shocked them as much as they shocked me. He kept talking and talking at me, not to me, and I shut myself down so tight I didn't hear another word he said. I watched his mouth move as if I were watching a silent movie.

It seemed like hours from the moment he started to the time he finished talking at me. I just stood there, staring at him, like a mute child. I had nothing to say to him, and a knock on the door interrupted the lecture. With relief, I watched as Mama grabbed our belongings and directed me out the door with a firm grip on my shoulders. She thanked Brother Thomas dutifully for his help on our way out the door.

Back in the car, I took a deep breath. All I could think about was going home to my room and my bed and pulling the covers over my head. At least that was safe, a safe haven for me.

The humming of the car's engine lulled me into a half-conscious state. It felt so good to be going home after that ordeal. In my semi-awakeness, I barely noticed the unfamiliar surroundings. Then I sat upright, fully alert now. This was not the way home and if we weren't going home, then where were we headed?

We came upon a large brick wall, fencing in an entire building. The wall seemed to stretch on for miles, its weathered red brick a pale dusty grayed pink. The wall looked huge, looming up beside the car, as if it would swallow us around the next bend in the road, or if we even veered an inch closer to it. I didn't like the feeling I had riding next to this wall. When we arrived at the end of it, a huge black cast iron gate met us. It had sharp, pointed spears at the top, guaranteed to skewer any one who dared to climb over it.

Mama came to an abrupt halt at the gate. Not one person was in sight.

"See this place, young lady?" It was a statement more than a question. I kept very still. She pointed at the gate and the large gray building behind it. "That's where they put girls like you who get out of hand. Girls who don't mind their parents."

I didn't say a word. Not one word would come out of my mouth.

"If that's where you want to live then just keep up your craziness and I'll make sure to put you in there and you won't ever get out. They keep this gate locked tight, and it's very well fenced. You could try to escape, but you wouldn't make it. No one does. So you better listen good to what Brother Thomas had to say today," she said in a low, menacing voice. I had never heard her quite so mean, so threatening before.

The pain was fierce now, and it hurt every cell in my body. Once again the car moved, but this time toward home. I just sat in my seat, frozen with pain, not able to speak. Every now and then I felt a sharp stab of energy when Mama glared in my direction. The feeling of betrayal invaded my body. I decided that I would never, ever trust her again. I'll lock my door at home when I'm with John or helping someone move on to the golden light. I refused to let anyone catch me anymore. I'd just have to be very careful from now on. Extremely careful.

Let go of sorrows past

for they bring in Tomorrow's

Woes

Embrace the essence of
the Here and Now

Where the river of life flows

CHAPTER FIVE

Energy

"Listen, if you want to sit here all day and mope around that's your choice. Personally, I would prefer to do something more constructive," John said a few weeks later, his normally patient attitude stretched to the limit.

I didn't respond, except with a non-committal shrug of my shoulders, indicating to him that I didn't care about his suggestion one way or the other.

"Wonderful," John stated with a frustrated snort, as he paced back and forth across my tiny bedroom floor. "Alright, I can understand your unhappiness where your family is concerned, but it's time to release your sadness and get on with your studies and your life."

"That's easy for you to say," I answered defensively, not moving from my position on the bed. "You weren't driven past a girls home yesterday and threatened to be put in it."

"Carol, one of the necessary things you have to learn in this lifetime is that not everyone can or is willing to accept where you are spiritually. Your mother is afraid when you talk about spirits in the house and she acts out of her fear. You just frighten her, that's all. Learn to keep quiet about what you see and what you learn from me, or you will experience more negative reactions from your family."

John paused to see my reaction to all he had said. I

nodded my head solemnly to show him how seriously I understood what he was saying. He continued, "This house looks hike a black cloud has settled down over it. Everything in and around the house has become dark and gloomy. It feels so bad here that I have a hard time staying in here with you. The dark and depression is like a heavy lead cloak, settling on my shoulders and forcing me to want to leave. Let's clean some of this negative dark energy out and get ourselves into a happier space."

"How? How can we do that?" I asked, more enthusiastic than I'd been in a long while. I felt better already just thinking about doing something to rid this gloom.

"Let's clean house and clear the negative feeling by visualizing," John began. He closed his eyes and began the instruction. "Close your eyes and feel yourself relax."

Immediately, I felt my body relax as a warm vibration flowed through me, beginning in my feet and slowly swirling up my body until I felt warm and relaxed all over. I could hear John's voice, soft yet firm, take me to the next step.

"Now, Carol, picture a large cloud of golden light above your head. See it vibrating with the golden energy," John instructed gently. I could see the beautiful golden cloud, bright and shimmering like the sun. "Now take a deep breath and breathe in the golden light. Fill your lungs to the brim with the light."

I expanded my lungs and gulped in the beautiful golden substance eagerly.

"Now, blow the light out into each room of the house. Blow into each room, filling it, until the entire house is full of the golden light."

I started with the kitchen and blew the lung full of golden light into it. As I moved from room to room, I breathed many deep breaths until finally the house was filled and no longer dark and gloomy. Now it shined brightly, and its brightness contrasted the still dark yard and barn. I took in another cleansing breath of golden light and blew it over the yard and barn area until they, too, shined brightly. I felt such a sense of light happiness inside me, because I knew the job had been completed. I slowly opened my eyes and took a look around my room. It felt different. Clean, clear, and free of all that gloom.

I felt different, too, as if I had experienced a refreshing bath from the inside out.

"Well, what did you want to do today?" I asked cheerfully, feeling at peace within myself and ready to take on this world, including the next.

"That's my girl!" John shouted with a clap of his hands. "I'm glad you feel better. To tell you the truth, I don't think I could have stood the negative vibrations running through this house much longer. Now, go do your chores to make your mother happy and wear some old torn-up clothes, because I have a place in the mountains I've been wanting to show you." With that final bit of information, John was gone.

I did as he instructed, choosing to wear an old pair of blue pants and a faded hand-me-down shirt. I ran down the hall to the kitchen, grabbed a few cold biscuits to eat as a late breakfast, fed the chickens and milked the cow. The morning had quickly melted into early afternoon by the time I had finished my work. As soon as I was done, I went to meet John at one of the old workshops near the house, where I knew I would be sure to find him.

"Ready?" John asked, lounging comfortably against the wooden door sill. His mind seemed a thousand miles away.

"Yes, I'm all finished here," I replied, wondering why his thoughts seemed so distracted. I asked him what he was thinking.

"Thinking?" John replied, walking down the two small porch steps to where I was standing. "Oh, let's just say I'm checking to see where we are going and if the coast is clear. Just follow me, and I'll tell you the rest when we get there."

It was a beautiful summer day, the sun was warm and

bright. We couldn't have asked for a more perfect day to be outdoors.

I followed John up a dirt road leading from our house into the mountains. After we had walked up the road for about two miles, John paused, turned off the road, and began to follow what seemed to be a small trail. I could tell, after walking a few hundred yards, that the trail we were following had once been an old logging road, now almost fully overgrown with brush and small pine trees. The brush gradually became thicker and thicker, until the road disappeared completely.

John, who had been walking faster than I and remained a few feet ahead, stopped at this point, turned to his right, and closed his eyes. I slowed my pace and walked to where he was standing. A small hint of a smile tugged at the corners of his mouth, illuminating his profile as I approached. Suddenly, he opened his eyes and pointed with his right hand to a new direction.

"This way!" he shouted, and began to follow an old animal trail which led higher up into the mountains.

The higher we climbed, the more dense and untamed the forest became. Pines, hundreds of feet high, towered above our heads and blocked the direct rays of the sun. The temperature dropped in the filtered sunlight and the cool air felt good against my skin. The undergrowth, I noticed, which had a few hundred years ago grown so profusely, tapered off almost completely. Pine needles instead of grass and bushes, carpeted the forest floor. Years of constant needle accumulation lay beneath our feet, muffling and erasing the steps of our passage. The sound of rushing water roared in the distance and within minutes we were standing near the bank of its source.

The forest dwindled into a large green meadow which hugged either side of the wide and fast flowing creek. Sunlight, held at bay by the large pines, now resurged, illuminating and warming the entire area, giving life to the yellow wildflowers woven delicately amid the lush green grasses. Everything here seemed touched with its own indescribable magic. From the trees, to the birds, to the rocks, and the clean, rushing water, everything we came in contact with seemed a part of some enchanting fairytale.

"We'll stop here for a minute," John decided, looking appreciatively around us. "Let's sit down so you can catch your breath."

John had been moving fairly fast and I welcomed the chance to rest.

"Where are we going?" I asked, as we sat down near the creek, interested in our destination.

"A secret place of learning," he replied with a smile.

"Where?" I asked with barely contained excitement.

"You'll see," he responded, his smile turning into a mischievous grin. "Don't be so concerned with tomorrow that you forget about today. In other words, enjoy what you are experiencing now, the rest you'll find out soon enough."

The conversation I could tell was closed, so I decided to do as John suggested and enjoyed my present state of being.

A subtle breeze had began to blow and I welcomed its cool caress on my face. It carried with it the scent of the pine and loving, growing things I found refreshing. My gaze wandered over to the wide, rambling creek which flowed a few feet in front of us. Golden flashes of sunlight, caught here and there in the water, sparkled as brightly as any evening star. Each flash lasted for only a second, and was extinguished as the water direction changed, only to reappear moments later someplace else. As I enjoyed my surroundings, the wisdom of John's advice became clear.

In my haste to pursue tomorrow, I would have missed the beauty of today, robbing myself of the essence of life. My reality of today would be sacrificed for my dream of tomorrow. So, in pursuing the dream we sometimes forget how beautiful and important the now is. Since I have learned that time doesn't exist, I know that in experiencing our reality we experience the dream. What is reality but a dream made visible? And what is today if it is not a part of tomorrow? What is tomorrow if it is not the reflection of today? Both today and tomorrow then are interchangeable. So are they the dreams of reality or the reality of dreams?

"What do you think?" John asked thoughtfully, eavesdropping on my internal dialogue.

"Dreams, reality, today and tomorrow are all the same," I responded without hesitation.

"Right, so why worry about tomorrow when it exists at the same time as today. When you live today fully you live yesterday and tomorrow fully as well. Enough of this for now. I can see you are well rested and ready to move on," John said, as he stood up from where we had been sitting and ceremoniously dusted a few pieces of grass away from his pants.

Within moments, jumping from rock to rock, John had led us across the creek and back into the forest. After we had climbed upward for what seemed like miles, almost scaling the summit, John stopped and asked what I saw.

I took a few deep breaths, steadied myself, and looked around. The area was beautiful. Great limestone boulders on my left skirted the side of the mountain up to what I believed must be the peak. Pine trees of various sizes grew in front of, and to the rear of where we stood. Some, in their determination, had lodged themselves into the face of the bare rock and grew straight and tall defying the need for soil, instead relying on the strength of the mountain to give them life. I looked above us and saw that the sky, except for a few wispy opaque clouds, was as clear and blue as a robin's egg. I was dazzled by the brilliance of the sky's blueness, but since I detected nothing unusual in anything I had seen so far overhead or to my left, I directed my gaze to my right.

The limestone made another resurgence of massive proportions. It jutted out along the side of the mountain like a large extended human hand, the palm open and receptive.

The fingers pointed outward and balanced in the space between the heavens and earth, the physical and spiritual, the mundane and sublime. Under this mountainous extension the lower hills and valley rested below. Where my house would have been was a mere speck in the distance, insignificant in relation to where I stood. It was as large in size as the blue bell-shaped flowers growing near the toe of my shoe. This put things into perspective. The greatest house or building on the earth was no larger nor greater than the smallest flower that grew wild in the fields. Nor was a man or woman more important than the tiniest hummingbird that flew silently in the air. Everything from the minute and seemingly insignificant, to the colossal and monumental carried the same weight and significance. Nothing was worthless in the eyes of our creators, the universal god and goddess-consciousness.

"What do you see?" John repeated, the golden light of the sun highlighting the soft hues of his blonde hair.

"Beauty," I whispered, not wanting to interrupt the melodious birdsong or the continuous wind chiming through the trees, allowing the sacredness and magic of the small clearing to overcome me.

"You have spoken truly, but tell me what else you see," John said, with a small flourish of his hands to the area around us. "This time look not with your physical eyes, but instead with your inner-mind's eye."

What was it that he wanted me to see? I pondered and closed my eyelids halfway, looking at the world through the soft eyes of my mind and higher self.

There it was, it had been right in front of me the whole time! How blind I had been!

"A cave!" I shouted, jumping up and down in excitement. "You wanted to show me the cave, right John?!"

"You get an A plus for your lesson today," John replied, almost as excitedly as I.

I ran over to the cave entrance as fast as my feet would

carry me. On closer inspection, I realized that the cave was more of a lean-to type of structure. A large flat limestone boulder had fallen from above eons ago and settled at a forty-five degree angle against the sheer wall of limestone I had seen to my right. The area was neither overly wide or deep, but would easily and comfortably fit two or three people.

"What are we going to do with this place, John?" I asked, turning to where John stood beside me.

"Simple, Carol," he responded with a grin from ear to ear. "We're going to make this into a school room, a private place for you to continue with your studies."

"It will do for now John, but I think it will be a little drafty in the winter time," I added, looking through to the open end of the lean-to cave.

"It will only need some work and tender loving care," John replied, bending down as he walked into the center of the cave.

I followed him quietly from behind, silently summing up the work which would need to be done. It didn't take me long to figure out that it would take some doing.

"Nonsense," John interjected as he sat down on a limestone boulder that rested against the stone wall. "Next time we come up here you can bring a saw and some rope and this place will be warm and cozy in no time at all. But instead of thinking about fixing our new place up, let's just sit and become quiet." I sat down as John instructed at his feet, the short grasses and warm dirt, dry and soft beneath me. "Let's allow our energy to become one with this place. This is how we will stake our claim on it and keep all the other creatures living near here to stay away."

I welcomed the rest after our long hike and turned to look at every angle of the hidden cave. I took in every boulder, each crevice, and every plant that I could see. I closed my eyes and began to visualize, allowing each molecule of the entire area to become firmly implanted and etched in my mind and soul. With every breath I took, I extended my energy outward, blending with my surroundings until I felt the cave and I were one.

"Pull back now, Carol," I heard John say quietly, unable to distinguish if he was speaking physically or mentally.

I was so accustomed to his telepathic communication that it didn't really matter. I gradually let go of my extended body and drew my energy back inward. Doing this, I became aware of my own physical needs. My bladder felt suddenly as if it were ready to burst.

"I've got to find a place to go to the bathroom," I said, getting up to my feet.

"Alright, but let's use this to our best advantage," he said, remaining seated. "Go outside and mark your area. First go to the north and mark the ground with your scent. Then in turn, mark an opposite direction until each of the four cardinal points, north, south, east and west are imprinted with your spoor."

I left John in the cave and walked out into the open, near the rock which resembled an open palm. I unfastened my pants and squatted down, wetting the ground as I took in the view below me. What a glorious sight!

"I make the mountain mine," I thought to myself, "and all other creatures stay clear, that is, unless I invite you." I stood up, pulled up my pants and turned around in a circle with my arms extended outward at my sides, marking not only my spot in the physical world, but in the universe as well. I stopped, facing the direction in which I had started, and took in a deep breath, letting it out as I brought my hands down in front of me in a bow. I gave thanks to the universe, the very life force itself. I repeated this ritual three more times as John had directed, marking the four cardinal points on my mountain. When I returned to the cave I found John sitting where I had left him, smiling.

"You're glowing, Carol," he said in his soft and melodious voice, his eyes filled with joy and understanding. "I believe you already knew what needed to be done and I was right. Actually, you have carried this knowledge within your higher self for a very long time."

"I realized it, John, as soon as I began the ritual," I confirmed, elated with this new discovery.

"Good, Carol," John said as he walked to where I stood outside the opening of the newfound cave.

John stopped walking as he neared me and looked at the area around us. The cool, light wind we had felt all day had reversed itself and had suddenly turned cold. It tugged slightly at our hair, gently pulling it in various directions.

"It will be dark soon," John said, interrupting the tranquil silence. "We better start back."

We both gave the area one more look before our descent into the distant valley below, a look filled with a reluctance to leave.

"Come, Carol," John responded to my gaze of longing, placing a warm arm around my shoulder, "we'll be back tomorrow."

Though we had walked miles up to the cave, it seemed a much shorter distance as we made our descent. It wasn't long before I was once again standing on the front steps leading into my home. I ate dinner with my family, helped with the dishes, and went straight to bed. The covers felt warm and soft around me, and I hugged them close beneath my chin. Before I knew it, I had drifted into a deep and tranquil sleep, tired and happy from the day's journey.

The next day dawned brightly and as soon as the chores were done, John and I were off again to our special place in the clouds. This time though, I had come prepared. I had packed a special bundle, complete with saw, rope and food.

When we reached the cave, the work went quickly. John pointed out small pine trees which I cut and helped him rope together to form a wall, or wind-break for the cave. We worked all day cleaning, fixing, and arranging. Our thoughts had been so focused and intent on the task at hand that the sky had begun to darken before I realized it was time to head back home. We were so elated with our progress, we reached my house in record time, our step light and unfatigued.

Once again, I ate my beans and went unquestioned to bed. I hoped this particular pattern of unnoticed absence would continue as I drifted aimlessly off to sleep.

Somehow though, when I awoke the next morning, finished my chores, and readied myself to leave for the mountains, I knew it was too good to be true.

"Carol, where are you going?" my mother asked from behind me, catching me in the act of leaving as I filled my pockets with a few hard biscuits I had found sitting on the counter of the kitchen. I stopped dead in my tracks, my body stiffening as I turned to face where she stood, the look of surprise evident in my eyes and easily read across my features.

"Uh, nowhere," I lied, the words awkward and hard to come by as I stuttered my reply.

"Nowhere?" my mother questioned quizzically, eyeing me with suspicion. "It seems then that you are in a very big hurry to get nowhere. I hate to ruin your plans, but since you were going 'nowhere' anyway, I need you to stay close to the house and help your brothers with the firewood. No wandering away until you're finished. Do you understand?"

I nodded my head in silent compliance and watched my mother as she left the room. I trudged out into the yard where my brothers were busy splitting and stacking the wood. The biscuits in my pockets were all but forgotten as I began to work, my appetite having been completely extinguished at the moment of my mother's parental act. After a while though, my mood began to brighten as I replayed the conversation over and over again in my mind. It was suddenly clear, due to my various rationalizations, that once my firewood duties were completed, all responsibilities to my mother were finished. With that thought in mind, I worked harder than all my brothers put together and finished my designated part of the work within a few hours. So, when nobody was looking, I dashed away from the house and into the hills without a second glance.

My heart and step were light as I made my way along the familiar path which lead to my secret cave. As I neared the little stream I had so often jumped across, my stomach began to grumble and I pulled out from my coat pocket one of the neglected biscuits I had stolen earlier and nibbled at it absently as I continued my ascent. Grey squirrels chattered and scolded from the trees, while others, disturbed from their chore of gathering nuts on the ground, scampered in all directions as I approached them while walking along the path.

I looked around from time to time, anticipating John's appearance, but realized I was alone, except for an occasional glimpse of Raa, whose figure, visible for only an instant at a time, kept pace with me somewhere among the tall pine trees which lined either side of the path I was traveling.

Finally, by mid-afternoon, I reached my secret place in the sky. John's greeting didn't surprise me in the least.

"My aren't we headstrong today?" he stated pointedly, as he sat near the entrance of the cave, a frown riding deeply on his normally smooth brow.

"They didn't need me at the house," I replied nonchalantly, with a shrug of my shoulders, adding, "besides, my work for the day was finished."

"I'm not saying that it wasn't," John replied, raising an eyebrow in my direction. "It's just that I want you to be aware and remember that sometimes it's best to keep quiet and play along with your family's games a little. It keeps them happy. It keeps you happy and it keeps me happy. So just remember not to rock the boat, so to speak, and everything will be fine. And speaking of your family," John stopped his sentence and stood to look into the interior of the cave. Changing his line of speech he said, "Come here, Carol, I have something to show you." He gestured toward the cave with his hand.

I walked over to where John was standing and was amazed at the alterations he had made to the cave by himself. Fresh pine needles had been lovingly gathered and formed into a sleeping pallet which rested securely against the right side of the cave wall. Near the far back of the cave a fire-pit had been dug. It was a foot or so deep and at least that size around, tiny pebbles of various sizes and colors circled its perfectly round perimeter. Air holes, I noticed, had been worked into the far wall, providing ventilation for the smoke produced by the fires we would burn during the winter months.

"Oh, John," I beamed, clapping my hands together with excitement, "it looks just wonderful!"

All the while I was thinking to myself about how easy it would be to run away from home and live here instead.

"Be careful what you set in motion, Carol," John remarked seriously as we surveyed his handiwork.

"What do you mean?" I queried innocently, knowing full well what he was saying.

"There's an old saying: Be careful what you ask for, because you may get it."

Well, I *could* live here, I thought defiantly.

Later that afternoon, as the sun began its downward descent into the western horizon, I sat quietly enjoying the view of the valley from the top of my mountain. The air, sweet with the scent of pine and growing vegetation, was cool against my face. I reveled in the sheer beauty of the nature surrounding me.

I felt John's presence behind me and I turned my head in his direction.

"What do you think is down there?" he asked, extending his arm and pointing his finger downward toward the ravine near the bottom of the mountain.

I looked to where he pointed.

"I don't know," I laughed. "Water, trees, birds?"

"Good guess, Carol, but I want to teach you today how to

answer my question without guessing."

I got up when he finished, dusted off the seat of my pants, and began to walk in the direction he had pointed, ready to get started on my new lesson.

"No, Carol, you don't have to go physically to the place I indicated. Instead, we're going to use our energy and mind to find out what's down there."

"How are we going to do that?" I asked as I walked back to where John stood.

One of his eyebrows arched questioningly, his face clearly communicated the message: You already know how to do this Carol, why must I show you? Coming to grips with the fact that it might be a good idea for a quick refresher course, he began his instruction.

"Pretend you are down in the canyon. Let your mind open up and your energy spread out over the floor of the ravine. After you have done this, tell me what you see and feel. That's easy enough, isn't it?"

It seemed simple enough to me. So off I went in mind to the bottom of the canyon. I looked around and saw a beautiful fast-running creek. It tumbled playfully over several large granite rocks and boulders. The entire area was wet and damp and green moss grew profusely everywhere. The small plant was happy in this environment and clearly staked out this territory as its own, covering most of the rocks and trees. The fresh, yet musty smell of water filled my nostrils. Turning my attention from the creek, I quickly spotted a young, brown rabbit sniffing around the golden, leaf-littered ground for some food. I pushed my mind out farther to get closer to the rabbit, and he lifted his head. It obviously sensed that someone or something was close by. Excited by what I was experiencing, I pulled my energy back, and returned to the place where I was sitting. I was quick to tell John everything I had seen and felt. He was delighted with my progress and suggested I practice this technique. Soon, he told me, it would come in handy where my brothers were concerned. John felt it wouldn't be too long before they would become curious and try to find out where I was going everyday. So, taking his recommendation to heart, I sat and played this new game for at least the next hour.

"John, can't you tell me when my brothers might be following me?" I asked, still concerned by his insight.

"I could, but I won't. You are on your own in this one,"he responded in a challenging tone. "If I'm always there to tell you what to do, how do you expect to learn anything?"

Regretfully, I had to admit he had a point. In an hour or so it would be dark, so I bid good-bye to John and started down the mountain. Night had fallen by the time I walked through the back door of my home and I grabbed some cornbread which was sitting in a basket on the kitchen counter, deciding to eat a quiet dinner alone in my room.

My family was still up and I saw them as I passed the living room. Nobody said a word, they just looked at me very strangely. It didn't take a genius to figure out they had been talking about me. As I continued walking to my bedroom, I heard my brother David say, "Why don't you just leave her alone. If she likes the woods and acts like a tomboy, let her." I smiled a silent thank you to David.

As I lay in bed, John's prophesy I knew was soon to come true. Well, if it was in my power I would never allow my brothers to find my secret cave. So, I used the instructions John had given me and sent my mind and energy out to the cave. I then allowed my mind to show me different ways of getting to my spot. By the time I fell asleep I had found several different trails to follow, each one getting me easily to my destination. The last thing I remembered before succumbing to peaceful oblivion was the sound of John's voice whispering, "Good job, Carol. Good job."

The next morning I awoke before the rest of the household and set out to the mountain. I decided to use one of the paths I had visualized the night before. It was time, I figured, to put my studies to the test. So I visualized the cave and drew a line from it, back to where I stood. I went through a wide, grassy field, strewn with the wildflowers of summer, and followed a creek for what seemed like miles. I stopped in my travels every so often to feel the presence of the cave and pin-point it in my mind. Once I was sure of my direction, I pressed onward. After some time I found myself standing in the ravine I had explored in mind the day before. I was elated! It looked exactly as I had seen it yesterday. I finally felt confident I was on the right track. I looked upward into the dense forest hugging the side of the mountain above me. I wasn't able to see the cave from where I stood, so I once again visualized it in my mind. From what I could gather it was directly above me, nestled high among the farthest treetops within my sight. So I pushed on, scaling the steady upward slope of the mountain within an hour. John was waiting for me when I arrived. This particular path was much longer than the one I had always taken before, but it had proved that if I first went to a place in mind and followed the lines originating from the source back to where I was, I could draw a map that was easy to follow. The rest of the day John and I discussed what I had learned and we talked, or I did, for a long while.

The day began much in the same way that most days had. I followed a completely different path, arriving early at the cave. John, as usual, was waiting there to greet me. He had it in mind to take a walk, so we started off around the side of the mountain. As we continued walking, he began to speak.

"Today we'll carry our instruction of the last couple of days a little further," he said, lifting his robe above his ankles and sandaled feet as he navigated around a particularly large granite boulder. "Walk as though you have feelers. Spread your aura, or energy body, far out and over a wide area around you and feel everything it comes in contact with. If you sense any unusual vibrations within your field of sensation, stop and ask yourself what it is."

I did as he instructed, sending my aura out in a wide area around us. Suddenly, I felt a strange vibration emanating from the area in front of us. I told John what I was feeling and we immediately stopped our walking. I asked my higher self what was causing the disturbance in my aural body. In an instant, the picture of a long, black snake sunning itself on an old log came to mind. John and I quietly stalked up to where I felt the snake would be. Much to my delight, the snake was exactly where I had seen it. What a beauty it was. Its black scales were so dark that they glistened a deep blue in places where the sun caught upon the ripples of its skin as it breathed. The snake's tongue was also black, and darted rythmically out of its smiling mouth. The snake was obviously trying to smell the air as it did so. We were content to watch the creature and admire its beauty this way for the next few minutes. John was the first to interrupt the silence.

"Now, Carol, I want you to form a gold ball of light, just a small one, in your mind's eye and place it in front of you."

It only took me a second to see a small gold ball dancing above the ground, mid-air, in front of me.

"Good. Now place this same ball of light into the snake's mind and connect your energy to it."

Alright, I thought, I'm connected.

"Perfect. Now take the light you placed inside the snake's mind and move it in any direction you would like the snake to go."

I visualized shifting the light from the snake's head into a thin golden line in front of the animal and drew a line that stretched a few feet across the ground, spiraled up around the trunk of a tree, and into one of the higher most limbs. To my surprise, the snake instantly followed the light across the ground, around the tree and into the limb, only stopping where the light trail had ended. I was ecstatic!

"You see how easy it all is," John said proudly. "Now you will be safe anywhere you go. Just remember to always walk with your psychic feelers out and you will be prepared for anything. Now practice what you have learned."

And I did. I practiced all the way down the mountain to my house. I felt the birds, played with the squirrels and laughed with the tiny field mice. By the time I reached my front yard, twilight had set in. Unwilling to give up my new game, I decided to continue my play into the night. I found the ground beneath an old pecan tree in our front yard soft with the carpet of green grass. I snuggled under the pliant brilliance of a thousand stars. Soon, overhead, the unmistakable calling of a few bats could be heard. Their high-pitched electrical sounding radar seemed to be originating from all around me. Suddenly I had an idea. I picked out a bat and connected with it in much the same way as I had with the snake, but instead of just visualizing a gold light in front of it, I used my index finger to draw a line in the air with the light, pointing in the direction I wanted the bat to go. I made big circles around the house and then back toward the tree. It worked! In wonder, I watched the flying bat as it circled the house three times, and returned to circling around the pecan tree, just above me. I couldn't help from laughing with delight.

David came out and asked me what I was doing. I told him about the light and showed him what to do. It wasn't long before we were both making circles of golden light, with bats following obediently behind.

Our laughter attracted another member of my family, our older brother, Mark.

"What are you doing?" he asked suspiciously, his tone surly and condescending.

Innocently, David explained what we were doing, further compounding the problem by asking him to join in.

"Don't let her suck you in, David!" Mark growled. "This is the work of the devil. Don't ever get close to her, she's an evil person!"

I had listened enough to Mark's insults and his distorted

way of thinking. We had been having a wonderful time until his arrival and now he was spoiling everything. I felt the anger rising, burning through my whole being, needing direction and release. I stood and turned to where Mark stood. All of my anger became oncentrated in the tip of my index finger and formed into a ball of churning, erratic red and gold light. I shot the entire mass of energy at him as I spoke, the air crackled and sparked with its intensity.

"Be careful where you put your foot, Mark, because you're stepping in places where it doesn't belong!" I shouted, leaving my two brothers behind as I walked off to my room in a huff.

I tried to sleep, but it was no use. I still couldn't shake the anger I was feeling. I got up, hoping some fresh air would help and went outside to sit on the back porch steps. I tried to play my new game with a few moths, but alas, nothing worked.

By the next morning my anger was completely released. I busied myself with getting dressed and finishing my chores of milking my cow, Betsy. This was the day for canning jelly, a busy day to say the least.

David, Mark, and Peter had spent the whole day before picking blackberries and the huge buckets of ripe, sweet-smelling berries awaited us in the kitchen.

After my chores of milking Betsy and feeding the chickens, I hurried into the kitchen, slipped into an apron, and awaited the hot, steamy process of canning. The heat from the old wood cooking stove mingled with the humidity rising steadily outdoors to create an almost unbearable working condition. Even with the heat, I loved canning. The picture of fresh jelly spread lavishly onto warm biscuits on the morning of a cold winter day filled my mind.

By mid afternoon, we had completely run out of sugar. And what good is making jelly without sugar? So, Mama sent me to the store to purchase ten pounds of the sweet substance. I welcomed the walk as I stepped from the steamy indoors into the cool breeze of summer. The two mile walk went quickly as I caught glimpses of Raa running stealthily through the bushes next to me. It felt good knowing I wasn't all alone on my walk.

After purchasing the sugar, I took quicker steps to get me home, with the realization that if canning were completed today, then tomorrow I would be free to sneak up to the mountains — suddenly, a sharp pain shot up my foot, traveling through my entire leg, throbbing with its presence. I examined my foot, but there was no reason for the pain, it looked normal. Yet it kept throbbing steadily, not at all ceasing the whole walk home.

Once inside the house, I heard garbled hysteria coming from Mark's room. I dropped the sugar where I was and went to see what the trouble was. As I neared his room, I heard Mark crying in pain, his wail disturbing to my ears. The sight of my mother tending to Mark's foot as he sat crying on the edge of his bed was the first thing I saw as I rounded the corner from the hallway. On closer inspection, I noticed two or three bloody towels had been heaped on the floor near my mother, as well as a bloodied board from which a stained and dirty nail protruded. My eyes went from the board and nail, to the contorted face of my brother.

I asked what happened, now realizing that the pain in my foot earlier had been Mark's pain, and not my own, that I had been experiencing.

"He jumped off the hay loft in the barn onto that board with the nail in it," David said, gesturing with his hands to mirror the event.

"It's a huge nail," Ricky added, grimacing with a shiver. He pointed to the bloodied nail, "It went right through his foot."

The sight of all the blood and the pain in my foot and leg suddenly made my stomach lurch. I started to feel woozy and faint, until I forced myself to pull together. I pulled energy through me and got myself grounded in my highest spiritual energy. This stopped my upset stomach. After I repeated several times that this was not my pain, I won't own this pain, the pain began to cease. The dizziness slowly disappeared and I was able to walk steadily back into the kitchen, back to where I had hastily left the sugar bags in the middle of the floor. I took up the canning where I had left off, silently visualizing Mark full of golden and green light to help him heal. As I stirred the bubbling purple mass of blackberries, I saw no longer purple, but green and gold, the image of working on healing my brother.

The guilt was overwhelming. So overwhelming, that for the next three days I worked on my brother. Somehow, I knew I was the one responsible for his pain. The image of the night David and I played with the bats loomed distinctively in my memory. I felt I caused the injury, I should also be the one to help heal it.

After spending three days trying to heal my brother, I decided to take another trip to the mountains for the day. On my journey John appeared and walked beside me, much to my surprise.

"Come on, Carol," he said, "Let's go over to the pond. I want to show you something."

I followed obediently, feeling the intense heat of the sun on my shoulders as we made our way to the pond that was about a mile away from our house.

When we finally reached the pond, we stood at its small, rocky bank and I noticed it was a cattle pond. Hoof imprints dotted the shallow edge, where they had once stood to refresh themselves in the cool water.

John picked up a large stone that was sleeping near the bank and cupped the rock in his hand, throwing it into the middle of the pond with one smooth toss. Upon impact, the rock created rings of water, miniatures waves rippled around the pond.

"Everything we do affects us, just like that stone I threw affected the pond," John said, speaking to me, but looking out toward the pond. "The deeper the thought and feeling, the more pronounced the splash and the larger the waves. Just think of your action like the stone's, the reaction of the splash and the consequence of the splash like the ripple which is felt throughout the universe."

As I watched the waves hit the bank, I noticed they started back toward the center of the pond, back to where they originated from.

"That's right, Carol," John said inside my head. "It all goes back to where it started from. That is the law of the universe: What you put out must come back to you."

He paused for a moment to let the information sink in. "Not only does your anger affect those around you, but it goes out to the world and then comes back to you. It may be from someone else that you receive this anger, but it's still your anger coming back to you.

"It's important to be responsible for your thoughts and feelings and put out only what you want to experience.

"You've learned a lot from this, Carol, and I'm proud of you. You stopped the flow when you grounded yourself and got in touch with your spiritual energy. Then you worked on healing Mark with loving energy, so stop feeling guilty about this, it's done. Look at the situation, learn and let go. Whenever feelings of guilt or anger, or any other unwanted emotion comes up inside you, take the time to stop what you are doing and take a deep, slow breath. Pull yourself into your center and fill yourself with love. Then release this love out into your world, coating it, so to speak, with your love."

I sat quietly next to John at the pond's edge, contemplating what he had just told me. After a while of silence, John asked me to fill myself full of pink light, because pink is the color of love and understanding. It felt like every cell in my body was being bathed in love. I felt the loving energy release from my body and cover my home, including everyone inside. An image of the house and its occupants painted pink with love filled my mind.

When I opened my eyes, I saw that the pond, too, was painted in hues of delicate pink. But this was the artistic work of the setting sun, gliding silently behind the mountains, softening the blue horizon and all it smiled on with a pastel blush.

The mooing cows beckoned to me, letting me know it was milking time. I stood up slowly, savoring my experience with John, like one savors a bit of sweet maple sugar on the tip of the tongue, and hurried to the barn to do my evening chores.

The words I speak
are
the diamond fields of my

soul

Jewels raw in form

my beliefs and feelings

shape the cut

They become faceted diamonds

Brilliant with light

Shining forth into my world

as life

CHAPTER SIX

Karma

The experience of intense love I felt with John at the pond lingered with me long after I returned home. With this feeling of love, I began to long to be a part of the life of my brothers and to feel the oneness of the family unit.

Silent and strong, I heard John's voice inside me, "Carol, put your energy into whatever you desire and you will have the experience in your life. But make sure that is what you want because that is precisely what you will get."

"Oh, yes," I said earnestly, without hesitation, "that's what I want, alright."

Lying in my bed, before going to sleep, I pictured in my mind's eye my brothers accepting me as one of their group. I felt my energy build inside me, then I let it all go. The thought, the energy, and the feelings of oneness all released into the world. I was then able to fall asleep, quickly and peacefully.

I awoke to the sounds of the Bobwhite's call, mingling with the baying of the cows, insisting they be milked. I hurried into clothes to start my morning chores. Before I knew it, the morning was quickly replaced by afternoon, the sun creating its customary hot and humid atmosphere. From a few yards away, the boys' voices drifted to me carried by the summer heat. Loud, boisterous talk mixed with hammering sounds came from out by the storage barn, so I followed the sounds, quietly sneaking up on the barn to get a closer look into their world.

I watched safely from a distance as they pulled apart one of the old wagons we had lying around the farm. The boys were intent on destroying the wagon so that they could rebuild it, fresh and new, more toward their liking. I felt a wave of empathy toward the old wagon friend, yet at the same time, a sense of excitement filled me as I realized it was a sort of rebirth for the old work wagon, for soon it would turn into a proud stage coach. Nonetheless, I heard its woeful groans with every new nail driven into its weathered frame.

The excitement in the boys' voices rose to an elevated level as they concocted a plan for all the boys in the neighborhood to get together and go camping in the woods with their wagons.

I silently watched and again wished to feel a part of their group.

Suddenly, Mark looked up and caught my stare. Seeing me, he pointed in my direction and, whispering in a voice only the circle of boys could hear, said something to make them turn and laugh at me.

Chants of "Girls can't camp", "Go away, you're a girl," and "You don't belong here" chorused out of their mouths, trying to frighten me with their stinging words, like a cat being chased by water.

I didn't need much convincing that I wasn't wanted there, so I slipped away from the barn and ran up to the safe haven of my room.

Back in my protective space, I once again pictured them all in a circle, hands joined, with me in the circle, a part of their experience. Determined, I put all the energy I could pull together into the picture, then I let it go.

Every morning and every night I worked on this image.

It was about a week later when it happened. I saw the boys all gathered around the old oak tree behind the house, sitting in a circle and talking intently. As I moved closer I could hear muffled words. I so desperately wanted to hear what they talked about, have them respond to me, talk with me, be a part of their group. I inched closer, fueled by my desire, and much to my surprise, Mark and Peter looked my way and called to me.

"Carol, come here," Mark called out, somewhat jovial.

"We want to talk to you."

They finally wanted to talk to me! I was elated! I hurried over to the group and settled in next to my brothers. At last my desire was actually coming true, a happiness I could barely contain pulsed through me as I listened earnestly to their latest scheme.

"Well, we've got to sneak up on them at night," Peter stated, scratching his head in thought.

"I heard they won't come near boys," Ricky chimed in, nodding his head to indicate me.

"You're right," Mark said solemnly. "I heard the same thing. They only come to girls." Then all heads turned in my direction.

"I don't know," Peter stammered. He was drawing in the dirt with a stick, obviously mulling over the idea in his mind. "I don't think Carol can do it."

"You're right," Ricky agreed. They spoke as if I wasn't sitting right there, amidst their group, one of them finally.

"Do what?" I interrupted their verbal contemplation of the subject excitedly. "Do what?"

"Do you know what a snipe is?" Ricky asked slyly.

"Not really," I replied honestly.

"They're real pretty birds that only come out at night. People pay thousands of dollars for just one of them. They're real tame and friendly, so they make good pets. The only problem is that they can only be caught by a girl. David thought maybe you could help us catch one," he finished waiting expectantly for my answer.

"Sure, I can do it," I said confidently, feeling very important all of a sudden.

"Okay, we'll give it a try," Ricky stated, almost reluctantly giving in.

For most of the week we made our plans. It felt good to be a part of the group and my feelings toward my brothers took on new dimensions. They bordered on friendship and something akin to love. Yet I felt something, something strange and one of those not-quite-right feelings, but I pushed it aside, after all, now I was a member of the group.

The night of the new moon arrived and we were ready. This time of cloaked darkness presented the best opportunity to catch the unwary snipe, since they were, according to my brothers, shy, nocturnal creatures, afraid of men and light. We stole out of the house after my mother was sleeping and sneaked out to the farthest field on our farm. The wind had picked up after the sun had gone down and chilled my hands and face, but undaunted I went on, picking my way across the field whose surface remained a mystery under the blanket of an unlit sky. Tufts of grass, rocks, and dirt clumps, felt but unseen, proved treacherous to our footing, more than once causing me to trip and lose my already unsteady balance. I could almost believe I heard these earthy objects laugh each time I stumbled against my brothers for support, but I didn't stop to listen, instead I continued plodding on.

Finally reaching our destination, my brothers handed me a large sack and told me to stay put. While it was my job to catch the snipes, it was their task to flush them out. They left me alone with the understanding that they would circle around the outermost fringes of the field, chasing all of the snipes in my direction. I whispered solemnly that I would get as many as I could, and that I wouldn't let them down. I could hear their unsteady footsteps for a few minutes, then all went silent. They left me then, all alone, blanketed under a canopy of glittering stars.

What seemed like an hour went by, then maybe two and still the quiet remained, broken only now and then by the scurry of a field mouse rattling among the dried grasses of summer, or the screech of a barn owl hunting in the darkness of the early morning sky. I watched the constellations cross the sky, and sat down on the damp earth, hugging my knees against me. By the third hour, my body shaking from the cold, I realized that if I waited for a hundred new moons I'd never catch a snipe. I knew, once again, that I was the butt of their cruel joke. Both my belief in snipes and my trust in my brothers had been unfounded, and I felt my anger begin to rise in my body. It wasn't the rocks I had heard laughing at me, but my brothers, and I cursed myself for my stupidity. I wanted to cry, but found I couldn't, the tears having dried with my anger. By the time I reached the house, love was the last thing on my mind. At this point all I wanted to get was even.

The next morning I was teased without mercy. If I heard, "Want to go snipe hunting?" or "Where are the snipes, Carol?" one more time I knew I was going to scream. But I bided my time, bit my tongue, and waited for the best possible opportunity for my revenge to present itself. I didn't have long to wait.

On a bright, warm afternoon, the plans for my brothers' wagon train extravaganza came to full flower. All the boys from the neighboring area came over to participate. They hitched up the horses to the "stagecoach" and headed up toward the mountains. I waited until they were almost out of sight and then began to follow. Half way up the mountain Raa joined me in pursuit, and I welcomed his silent companionship. The boys soon made camp in a clearing near a stream, and I was careful not to be noticed. As soon as night fell, I climbed high into the boughs of a tree and settled in, watching and waiting for the boys to fall asleep. My moment of triumph had arrived, and I began to vocalize my anger and pain in animal sounds which I hoped would send fear into even the most brave of campers. Raa followed suit and added guttural growls and roars to my eerie repertoire. One by one, the boys awoke, wide-eyed with fear and took off on foot down the mountain, against Ricky's protests. My brothers, the last to leave, huddled together for protection, and calmed down the nervous stamping and whinnying of the horses just long enough to get inside the wagon. After they were out of sight, the wheels of the wagons and fearful step of the horses no longer audible, I climbed out of the tree, and sat down at the base of it. I began to laugh so hard, remembering the frightened expressions of my brothers, that I cried. All the way home, under the protection of a full moon, I giggled to myself with well-founded glee. The chill that bit at my feet, hands, and face only proved a small irritant, having been warmly wrapped in my cloak of satisfactory revenge.

The next morning, smiling, I asked my brothers if they had fun on their camping trip. With averted eyes, they informed me they had a wonderful time, but their mumbling tone belied their true emotions. Nothing more was ever mentioned about the wagon train experience by my brothers. Only I knew the reason why. I made a point not to bring it up, knowing that now the score had finally been evened. I also realized that I really didn't wish to be a part of their unit anymore, it was evident they lived in a completely different world than I.

Summer was now in full bloom. In all these months of spring and early summer, my chores and work had kept me from my mountain. The need to get away began to consume me, and I waited for the day I could get up before the rest of the household and sneak away. My brothers would have to do my chores today, I decided, pulling the covers away from my bed. It was still dark so I fumbled in the morning twilight for my clothes, finally finding a lost sock beneath the bed. Tiptoeing down the hall, to the steady breathing of my sleeping family, I made my escape out of the back door. The sun had just begun to light the cobalt sky and chase the stars away, when I made my descent down the back stairs. The air was warm and heavy, and I knew that before long it would be hot as well. Bobwhites chimed in the distance, announcing my arrival, as I reveled in my newly acquired freedom. Everything around me smelled new and fresh, yet something seemed amiss, something I couldn't quite place. I dismissed this feeling as excitement and continued on my way.

About half way up the mountain, as I crossed over the slow running mountain stream, I fell and bruised my knee, something I'd never done before. I shrugged it off, and chided myself to pay better attention, then continued with my ascent. Soon, moving up the ravine, I could see the large, grey rock formation which marked my home in the mountains. It rose above the peaks of the pine trees, like some giant sentinel, beckoning and calling me home. It was more of a home than the one I had left behind me. That was my mother and brothers' house, this was undeniably mine. I scrambled over the last few boulders and steep ledges separating me from my destination, and paused to catch my breath. A few yards upward, I could see John standing at the base of the great monolith, grinning and waving his hand. I raised my hand in reply, laughing out loud as I ran the last few paces to greet him.

In his big, warm bear hug I felt happy. Happier than I had been in months, for this was my *real* family. After a minute or so, John, his hands gripping my arms, gently pushed me out to arms length. He looked over my body from head to toe, his eyes intent and searching. Dropping his hands away from my arms, he began to make a peculiar movement around me. It was as if he was pulling something out from inside of me, uprooting the seeds of something planted deep within my soul. After a few moments of this strange new ritual, I asked John what he was trying to do.

"Take an educated guess," he said with a bit of surprise, continuing to pull at whatever was embedded within me.

As I concentrated I became more aware of a bizarre

sensation, that of having strings tugged away from my body.

"I thought you'd feel it sooner or later," John stated, noticing the expression of disbelief suddenly washing over my face. He chuckled over my discomfort, then continued. "You've been busy lately, haven't you? Haven't seen this accumulation of negative energy in a while."

He laughed again, this time in reaction to my blank expression, and continued at his spiritual tug-o-war.

"You've been letting your anger get away with you," he said reproachfully, changing his carefree mood, nodding his head from side to side in admonishment. "You allowed your family's negative vibrations to get attached to you. You look like a spider has spun its web throughout your aura making it dark and dirty."

I couldn't think of anything to say in reply. I knew he was right, but it didn't make me feel any better at the moment. I just watched in silence as he continued to clean away the web I had tangled myself into.

"You see, Carol, each one of us is standing in the center of our own universe, moment by moment creating the tomorrows of this lifetime and the next. The earth is the place of works. This work is the product of our thoughts, actions, emotions, and dreams, whether we are conscious of it or not. You've been busy building a strong web of pain and anger, a web I've just finally finished pulling away."

"Thanks John," I humbly replied, feeling strangely lighter than I had when I first arrived.

"No thanks needed. Just live by what I've taught you. It will save you a lot of trouble later on," he replied with a warm grin, one eyebrow impishly raised, alerting me all was well. "Come on, it's time you work on yourself. Let's go for a walk down to 'the pretty places'."

I smiled in reply and took his hand in mine. I loved 'the pretty places', so dubbed for its beauty and majesty. My step felt lighter than it had in months, and I skipped at John's side as he walked. The sun had already begun to climb the horizon, warming the world below, but in the forest, under the protection of the large pine trees, it remained cool and comfortable. I breathed in deeply the intoxicating fragrance of pine permeating the air, and listened to the birds' songs coming from all around us. The sound of waterfalls, roaring in the near distance, alerted me that we had almost reached our destination, causing me to run ahead of John to the open pine grove a few feet in front of us.

The sight which greeted me was spectacular. Large slabs of dark grey, mossy granite jutted out in a series of layers up against the steep incline of the mountain, causing the clear mountain water to fall in a glassy cascade from ledge to ledge. Here and there in places, large, pointed natural crystals protruded and lay embedded in the dark granite stone, the largest ones catching rivulets of spray, sunlight, and water on their clear faces, flashing prisms of color to where I stood. Instantly soothed by the sight of water falling over rock and crystal, I sat down upon the grassy bank and took in the view, awaiting John's arrival.

"Beautiful, isn't it?" John said coming up behind me.

"Yes, it is," I replied, still hungrily taking in the view.

"I want you to lay down here near the bank so that the water will be right next to your side," John began, waiting for me to comply, which I quickly did. "Good. Now try to feel the flow of the water, as if it were going over, yet through you."

After a few moments of quiet, I relaxed into the experience.

"Now take a deep breath through your nose and hold it to a count of four. Good, now open your mouth and breathe out, let it go. Once again, another deep breath, count to four, let it go. Now begin to feel the anger in your body."

Almost on cue I felt my anger surface throughout my body. Surprisingly, I had thought it was gone but I realized with each new wave that pulsed through me that I had buried the emotion deep within, where it lay hiding and seething, waiting for an opportunity to burst forward into the world around me.

"Now, Carol," John continued, sitting down near me on the bank, "make a fist with your hands, take a deep breath and push all the anger you are experiencing into your fists. Hold it there. Exhale slowly as you open your fists and let it go. Let all the anger go. Good, now clench your fists again and repeat the experience on your own."

I did as John instructed and felt all of my anger drain through my hands. It seemed as though a burden of unfathomable weight was flowing from my body. I smiled with eyes closed, enjoying the sensation and the feel of the sun on my face. I took another deep breath, not to extinguish my anger since it was all gone, but to take in fully the smell of pine and water around me.

I repeated the same exercise to rid myself of guilt. I took a deep breath, channeled the unwanted emotions into my fists, and exhaled, opening my fists and releasing all of the guilt I harbored. After I had finished, John continued.

"Now, listen to the water flowing clean and clear over the rocks. I want you to get into the water, lie down, and in your mind's eye let the water flow through you and cleanse you. Water represents the spirit, so feel your spirit flowing through you, clearing and cleansing you of all negative feelings and thoughts. Feel the flow of the water and spirit as it cleanses your entire being. Let go . . . let go . . . let go."

I did as John instructed and got into the water, feeling it gently flow over and through me. At first I felt refreshed and renewed, the coolness of the water feeling good after our long walk, but then, all of a sudden, the current in the water became so strong that it felt as if I was being pulled out of my body through my feet. The current became stronger and stronger, pulling at me harder and harder until I could no longer control the fear welling up within me. I was so afraid of disconnecting with my body, flowing down the river, and becoming lost forever, that I refocused my energy and immediately pulled out of the entire experience.

"Ha!" John laughed, knowing what I had done. "What a chicken! Don't you trust your higher self yet?"

I opened my eyes and sent him a lethal look, not enjoying his latest barb.

"Okay," he replied still smiling, holding his hands up in front of him in a gesture of informal surrender, "bad joke, but in order to finish cleaning the karma already set in motion around you, you must wipe the slate clean. The water can do this for you. Understand that water is the symbol for spirit, and the crystals, which the water is running over, symbolize the inner-self, or spirit, becoming solid form. The water is flowing over you, cleaning your emotional self and bringing the light of spirit through you in order to cleanse the inner-self. This way, once the negative energy has been removed we will fill you with love and pure, perfect form."

"Alright, I think I understand now," I said a little sheepishly, realizing I had been under John's protection during the whole meditation and had nothing to fear.

"One other thing," he added, raising his index finger to make a point. "In order to erase all of the past karma you must learn to love both yourself and your brothers."

"Loving myself is easy, but my brothers?" I exclaimed in exasperation.

"I know it's easy to love the people who are close to you and kind, but the true test comes about when you learn to love those who have hurt you."

"Why do I have to do all the work, while they do nothing?" I asked, a little put out about the whole situation.

"It's not them we're concerned about. They set their own life in motion. You need to keep yourself clear so that you won't be ignorantly sucked into their space."

My expression told him that I still wasn't convinced.

"Let me put it this way," he began, taking note of my feelings. "We live our lives within a large bubble. This bubble is a mirror that reflects everything we think and feel back to us. This reflection of our projections creates our own personal world. Anything can be projected onto this mirror covering the inside of your bubble. All people have their own mirrored bubble. Just remember you don't have to attach yourself or be a reflection in someone else's mirror. Do me and yourself a favor. Stay out of your brothers' bubble!"

"Okay," I answered with determination, "I'll really give it a try."

"Good," John replied with a smile. "Now, let's try the meditation again." He paused for a moment taking in the look of fear shadowing my face. "This time though, we'll change things a little for you. You won't be able to feel the pull of the water at all."

Relief exchanged places with the fear. I went to sit on a cluster of crystals John had motioned to and made myself comfortable. In this position, with my face and body bathed warmly in sunlight, I began the meditation again. I easily drifted into the experience, guided by the dulcet tones of John's soothing voice, soon passing through both the phases of karmic release and cleansing. This time though, when I felt spirit beginning to flow through me there was no sense of fear, instead it felt as though the warmth of the sun touched and revitalized every part of my being. The crystals beneath me connected with the light coursing through my body and began to radiate their own waves of light and heat. From far away, or so it seemed, I heard John telling me to visualize all of my brothers, smiling, happy, and active.

"See them all together, Carol," he said. "See them celebrating their birthdays together and watch them receiving, each in turn, great, beautiful, and wonderful gifts. Now visualize them all standing with their gifts in the middle of a giant, golden balloon. Send them love, Carol, and release them. See their smiles of joy and happiness. Now, watch as the balloon lifts from the ground. Allow this balloon with your brothers to float away from your sight. Wish them well as they disappear and send them all the love you feel in your heart."

I felt at peace and relaxed. The burden I had been carrying had been miraculously lifted. The weight of guilt and anger had disappeared with the balloon, leaving me happy and free. John and I sat side by side for a long while in blissful silence, watching and listening to the waterfalls dancing gracefully over the sparkling crystals. I felt completely at peace and at one with the world.

John and I began to talk. We talked about the meditation, the cleansing, and the peace I felt within my soul. The sun was beginning to set, so we settled ourselves on a ledge overlooking the valley and reveled in the natural spectacle unfolding before us. Ribbons of orange and red streaked intensely across the sky, then were extinguished as the sun disappeared below the purplish horizon.

The days passed quickly after the cleansing, as if what I had been carrying around had slowed me down immensely, and now I was moving quickly, unburdened and free. I felt the experience still working inside me every day as I worked around the house, readying it and ourselves for the coming winter.

I awoke as the first rays of the morning's golden light, unhindered by drawn curtains, flooded the expanse of my small room. In the distance, far outside my window, I could hear the Bobwhites softly calling to each other, filling the warm morning air with their quieting melody. This was my favorite time of the day and I reveled in every part of it. This was the time when I could meditate fully, without interruption, on my previous night's dreams and present day realities.

The comforting smell of cooking biscuits and coffee permeated the air and I smiled in satisfaction as I stretched my arms slowly behind my pillowed head. The covers felt warm and soft and I snuggled deeper into its great expanse, feeling safe and happy within my handmade cocoon.

Thoroughly relaxed and centered, I began to reflect on last night's dreams. John had made a point of discussing my dreams with me each time we met, and as such I kept a careful record. I had found, with John's help and instruction, that the dream state was actually a reflection of my conscious, outer reality. By paying close attention to what was happening within myself, I could easily understand what was in movement around me. Both the conscious and unconscious state were interchangeable and inseparable, being only a continuation and reflection of each other. This was an important lesson I had learned on more than one occasion, much to John's unabashed delight. I closed my eyes, allowing all other thoughts and sounds to depart from my conscious mind, and soon my dream came back in a rush of vibrancy.

I found myself flying through the inky darkness of the universe. In an instant I had flown past stars, planets, and other worlds to a place I had never been before. Gliding, unhindered by gravity, over a forested glade of evergreens, I began to slow and descend as I neared an open glade between the trees. Twinkling lights from fireflies adorned the trees, making it seem as if the stars themselves had fallen from the sky to decorate the world below. The smell of wood and pine heavily perfumed the air and I breathed in the pungent freshness as my bare feet touched the dewy lawn. The sound of high-pitched singing and giggling interrupted my quiet reverie and I turned my attention toward the center of the clearing where a large group of small children or elves were gathered. Though only as tall as my knee, they were perfectly proportioned in all ways. From the top of their shocking orange hair to their tiny well-formed bare feet, they cut a charming figure. Their clothing, if you could call it that, was unlike any I had seen. It resembled something akin to fabric yet was not cut in any particular design, instead it was artistically wrapped around each little person with a flair of individuality and care. The sudden thought of swaddling clothes or funeral shrouds quickly crossed my mind, but was soon dispelled as two of the diminutive figures suddenly stopped what they were doing, abruptly looked my way, and pulled away from the group and began to skip toward me. Giggling to each other and linked hand in hand, I could discern that one was male and the other female. I was struck by the roundness and enormity of their soft dark eyes, and was easily caught in their penetrating gaze. An unknown fear of these little people began to swell within me as they came closer. Although they extended their arms to me in greeting and friendship, it almost became too much to bear. Deep within their eyes I could detect some secret knowledge, or understanding, of which I was not privy. I realized they had been forewarned of my arrival and had somehow expected me, and I knew right away that this unrevealed knowledge was the basis of my uncontrollable fear. With a look of reassurance and another giggle, each took one of my hands and began to lead me back toward the center of the meadow where the group was still assembled. My desire to escape the situation was futile as I soon found I was unable to move away from the direction where they were leading me. As soon as I arrived with my tiny escorts at our destination, the group erupted into peels of laughter as they sensed my growing panic. Some shrugged their shoulders, others extended their hands, while still others shook their heads and stroked their beards, but all smiled as if to suggest reassurance and welcome. This simple overture of kindness slackened my anxiety somewhat and I felt free to look further around the area, an action I found I had previously been unable to do because of my feeling of panic. Though this feeling of false security was soon short lived.

There, near the outer fringes of the elfin folk circle, sat a dark rectangular shape. Black as deepest ebony, reflecting no light or shadow, it sat alone and beckoned for me to come. All my old fears resurfaced in heart-rendering crescendo, shaking my body uncontrollably. I tried to fly but could not, my feet rebelled and held me fast to the ground. The group laughed once again and smiled as two small figures summer-saulted toward the dark object and effortlessly lifted away its heavy lid. Golden light streamed magnificently from the box as soon as the lid was raised, pulsating with life and warmth. Strangely compelled, I was drawn to the bright light and inky darkness of the yawning tomb. I walked steadily toward it and climbed inside. As soon as I was settled within the casket, the lid was closed above me. All panic and fear were quickly erased from my being as I dwelled secure in my aloneness. I closed my eyes as I felt the golden light begin to swirl around me, caressing my spirit and limbs as it enveloped me in its soothing love. In moments the lid was lifted and drawn away and I begrudgingly climbed out of the confines of the black box to stand next to a beautiful woman radiating an aura of clear gold. She smiled in greeting and extended an outstretched hand which I immediately took and grasped. It was at this point that the dream ceased in clarity and lulled quietly into a haze of nothingness.

Now back in my room, in present reality, I reflected on what John had told me during one discussion we had up in the mountains about flying in the dream state. I remembered that he said it signified a passage into an inner-dimension, or leaving my body and entering into spirit realm. These inner-dimensions, or spirit realms, were so innumerable to our way of thinking that the human mind would boggle if confronted with such vast complexity. Only, he said, when approaching this topic from the rationale of spirit could we ever begin to fathom and comprehend the concept of inner-dimension and travel.

Well, regardless of a potential "mind boggle", I wanted to know where and why I had traveled to such a strange place and been an active participant in a bizarre ceremony I still couldn't quite comprehend. Too many questions had been raised by my experience and I was determined to learn everything I possibly could about it. I made a mental note to ask John about my nocturnal adventure as soon as I had the chance.

I was soon out of bed, brushing my hair, and quickly

dressed by pulling on a pair of old blue pants and worn socks and shoes. I raced into the kitchen where I greedily devoured a hot biscuit spread amply with thick berry jam and melted butter. This I soon topped off with a glass of cold milk after which I raced out to the barn where the cows impatiently waited to be milked, all bellowing in a loud voice of unified agitation.

I smiled as I walked, enjoying the gentle warmth of the morning sun on my face, while inhaling the intoxicating fragrance of new life that blossomed around me.

"Hello, Mr. Bird," I said in greeting to a friendly sort of chap who sat chirping above me on a newly budded branch. "How are you on this fine morning?"

He turned a small beady, yellow eye in my direction and continued to sing. I smiled, accepting his joyful reply, nodded my head in silent acknowledgement and turned toward the barn, where with some effort I opened the heavy barn door.

The musty smell of hay and manure, cows and grain filled my lungs as I closed the door behind me. It wasn't a bad smell, rather a pleasant one, which always brought on a collage of feelings centering around home, warmth, and security. I picked up the old tin milk-pail sitting near the door and made my way through the melancholy chorus of milk cows flanking either side of the old barn. I found my cow, Betsy, in her stall waiting patiently. As I approached her with my pail, she turned her soft, brown eyes in my direction and bellowed in recognition and gratitude. It wasn't long before I had her fed and grabbed a wooden milking stool from against the wall and positioned it next to her tethered form. I then placed the tin pail beneath her full udder.

Betsy and I had a wonderful understanding. I promised to feed her grain and she reciprocated by giving me her milk. I rested my cheek against her warm, hairy side and gently reached her soft teats. The milk soon came in quick, well-directed squirts into the pail, frothing and lightly steaming. I began to breathe as the cow breathed and soon our energy

connected together as one. We both relaxed into the
meditation as my hands worked automatically to fill the pail
with warm, sweet milk. Everything else in the world ceased to
exist except for the rise and fall of our breathing and the
consistent, dull sound of the milk squirting against the tin
pail.

I allowed my thoughts to drift back to my dream. I saw
the lid of the black casket drop and then lift. It closed on life,
then opened to a new one. Death and life were interchangeable. The casket was both womb and tomb. And I
realized, in that moment, that I had died in my dream, but
had been profoundly reborn to a higher spiritual understanding and knowledge. Yes, this is what the dream had
meant! My old self, heavy with the pain and fear of Carl and
loss of life, had died and in its existence a new self was born.
Like the Phoenix, my soul had withstood the fear of death
and had risen in triumph from the ashes of despair only to
be made complete, whole, and free in its new existence. It was
as if I had awakened from a deep, troubled sleep of
ignorance into a state of euphoric enlightenment. I knew,
without doubt, that everything I had learned in the last few
years had culminated in this single moment. I realized that
my father's death and my need to work with the spirits in love
and devotion were both necessary teaching experiences in
which I learned that death was not something to fear but
instead a part of life I needed to embrace and understand.
Death was not the ending, nor was birth the beginning,
instead they are both beginning and end, a circle, complete
and whole, never ending or beginning.

With this acute understanding of life and death, I felt a
spark of light descend through my head and down my spine,
sending armies of goosebumps throughout my entire body. I
felt alive and vital, almost electric, knowing I had touched on
a universal truth of spirit.

Utterly lost in my excitement, I had forgotten about
Betsy, who began to jump and kick so wildly that she nearly

knocked me off my stool. It took some time, but after a few gentle words and soothing strokes, Betsy finally settled down.

The episode with Betsy brought another universal truth to the forefront. It didn't take much to realize how interlocked everything on the planet really is. I am not alone in what I feel, nor is anything or anyone else. I knew without a doubt, after Betsy's reaction to my energy, that what I experience, Betsy experiences and what I feel, she also feels.

As I finished the last of my chores, I could hardly contain my growing excitement. The anticipation and need to tell John of my recent discoveries were almost more than I could bear.

I ran up the hill to the top of my mountain. The sky, a canopy in hues of white and grey, threatened at any moment to release its heavy burden of water from a summer rain upon my head, causing me to scramble even faster up the hill towards the protection of my lean-to cave. As I approached the summit, the blue robed figure of John became visible. He stood alone on the rocky ledge which jutted out above the distant valley like a silent warrior, his face drawn taut against the wrath of the cold breeze. A strong gust of wind suddenly replaced the breeze and pulled at his golden hair, creating a halo of locks behind his head. His blue robe whipped mercilessly about his legs, slapping and cracking the air behind him like a derelict flag. For some reason I was hypnotized by the spectacle, and stopped my running to admire the picture of blue robe and gold hair against the natural backdrop of deepening grey. John turned toward me as I approached and smiled in greeting, leaving whatever he had been thinking far behind him. I waited for him to join me and tried to catch my breath, my lungs burning in protest from the assault of cold air I drew raggedly and persistently through my throat. I began to excitedly tell him about my dream and my experience with Betsy. John listened intently while I told him about my dream and what I had learned about birth and death, and how Betsy felt my spark of energy.

I talked nonstop for some time about how life is always never-ending, it never stops being. When I finished running off at the mouth, more from lack of breath than lack of words, John looked at me for a long moment and then turned his focus out over the mountains.

He then began to share with me his thoughts. "Your cleansing experience the other day, at 'the pretty places', is continuing to be felt on inter-levels of your soul. Your dream released your fear even deeper than I would have thought. You are cleaning out lifetimes of fear which will allow you to take charge of your life with even more confidence." He paused in his explanation, thinking carefully about his next words. "Let's reflect on the experience. The time spent reflecting to understand an experience is just as important as the experience itself."

We sat on the edge of the rim looking down over the valley spread out below us. We felt a oneness with the earth and all at once, the dream and the cleansing became a part of my inner psyche, a lesson, I realized, that was well learned.

Ever changing circles

spiraling upward

through the illusion
of
space and time

circles of life
no ending or beginning

expanding growing

discovering the spiritual essences

by shifting and changing

Being
circles of life divine

CHAPTER SEVEN

Balance

It was an early rise now that school had begun. Although the sun outside my tiny bedroom window shined brightly, beckoning me outdoors with its warming appearance, I knew that fall was officially here. The sun was a deception to the chill that had permeated the air, and my numb fingers in the early morning hours struggled to button the sweater that fall insisted I wear.

My chores, as always, still had to be completed before leaving for the bus. I moved quickly through my tasks, my body functioning automatically while my mind was off in far away thoughts. This particular morning was colder than it had been, the milk from Betsy landed in frothy foam, steaming as it hit the ice cold bucket. I really didn't want to go to school, so the closer it came to the time to leave for the bus, the more I dragged my feet to work on my chores. The scattering of feed for the chickens seemed to take hours, or so I pretended, the feed falling from my palm in slow motion, the dipping into the feed bag at a snail's pace, the carrying of the milk into the house took years. I dilly dallied so much, Mama finally had to call me to hurry up. She was straining the milk through cheese cloth to get it ready for the milkman to pick up soon, and she needed my milk to complete her task. At the urging of her irritated voice, I picked up my pace, and after a quick face and hand wash, I knew there was no more stalling, I had to leave for school.

Like a prisoner sent to her execution, I trudged slowly toward the ominous bus stop, my head down, my books barely contained in my lifeless grasp. As I neared the bus stop, I took one last look over my shoulder, back toward my mountain home. I'd have much more fun there than at school any day, I thought defiantly to myself, and I'd learn much more, too. I'd learn important things, things that mattered to me, not some dumb math and reading assignments and all those boring subjects I was forced to understand in school. Right in the middle of my mental argument, I stopped walking toward the bus, and turned around to head toward the mountains instead. I needed no further convincing that this was where I belonged, fit in most, and loved more than anything, especially school. I didn't need school anyway, because the teacher always made me feel stupid, the students didn't even like me, so why even go there? The reasons were stacking up mile high about why I didn't need to go to that prison they called school.

I climbed through the sagging fence and went into the thick, brushy woods so no one would spy me escaping. I almost felt like a fugitive, sneaking away, moving stealthily through the brush, excited from doing what I wanted to do rather than what everyone else demanded of me. My heart was pounding both from the excitement and the physical exertion of climbing up the mountain. I knew I was on the right path to a very fun and eventful day with John and Raa.

The faster I climbed, the warmer I felt, and the morning sun, which had teased me earlier in my room to come out and play, suddenly felt warm and wonderful. I loved the outdoors. I sent out my energy feelers, like John had taught me to do and I felt something up ahead. Silently, inside my head, I asked what I was feeling. A picture of a turkey came into view inside my inner-eye. I slowed my pace and moved carefully so that I could sneak up and see for myself if I was right or not. I came upon a small clearing where two turkeys were scratching the frozen dirt for food. I pulled my energy back and sealed it off by wrapping myself in golden light which made me invisible to the turkeys. I stood there enjoying the two turkeys scratch and peck and rub against each other. They didn't suspect a thing as they carried on with their movements. Satisfied with my work, I moved up the mountain again toward my make-shift home. In no time I found myself up at the top and sure enough, John was standing there waiting for me with Raa lying on a gray boulder, licking one of his huge paws with the lazy urgency that all cats have. Every cell of my body radiated with energy at the sight of my two friends, I knew I had made the right decision to come here. My smile stretched from ear to ear in my happiness.

"Well, I felt you this morning, thought you were going to skip school and come up here, and here you are," John said very seriously with a strange look in his eyes. My smile slipped from my face, and in its place came a defiant set to my mouth.

"I just couldn't make myself go to school," I said harshly. "I learn so much more from you, John. Why, just a few minutes ago I made myself invisible and stood right next to a couple of turkeys. They couldn't even feel me much less see me. They don't teach things like that in school, John. It's so boring!" I was talking so fast I could hardly catch my breath, but I forged on, intending to say everything that was on my mind today. "I'm forced to read and do math that I don't even really understand, and my teacher acts like I'm stupid 'cause I don't catch on as quick as the other kids, and the other kids, they all hate me, I have no friends . . ." I stopped my breathless intense rambling. "Why do I have to go to that old school anyway?" I asked finally.

John stood there and just looked at me, not making any comment on all I had just said. "Looks like you need to put on your coat or go inside. It's really cold out here. Looks like one of those early winter storms coming in today."

I looked up and sure enough, the sun which I believed felt so warm earlier, had disappeared behind the approaching black storm clouds. I hurried into the cave where a warm fire greeted me, dancing in the make-shift fire pit we had built last summer.

John and Raa followed me silently into the cave, Raa moving to the farthest corner away from the intense heat of the fire. John stood next to me as I warmed my hands over the hot flames. I hadn't realized how cold my hands were until the heat started to thaw them out. Now I realized it wasn't the sun that warmed me as I made my way up the mountain, but my own body heat from the physical exertion of the climb.

An uneasiness invaded the room, I felt uncomfortable because I knew John wasn't too happy with me about the school thing. His look told me everything I didn't want to know, and his aura had red streaks throughout his customary beautiful deep blue. I knew that red meant he was upset. I continued to warm my hands, and as I did, I felt John's energy moving around my head. I knew he was reading my thoughts, so I put the thoughts really loud in my head. "You're my teacher," I said silently, "not the people in school."

All of a sudden, John burst out laughing. He laughed so hard, tears came to his eyes, and Raa woke with a startled expression.

"What's so funny?" I demanded.

"You just think you know everything, don't you young lady?" John said, trying to be stern, but not quite pulling it off with his bouts of laughter in between words.

"What do you mean?" I asked, fully perturbed now.

"Well, look at you, you can feel when I'm reading your thoughts. You can make yourself invisible, you read my aura. But Carol, tell me, how are you going to live in the world around you if you can't read or write or figure out how to handle your money? You're in this physical world, dear, whether you like it or not, and you have to learn how to live and survive in it. School is important, so you must change your attitude toward your teachers and see the learning process as one that's good for you. Stop resisting what you don't like or aren't comfortable with." He finished his lecture and looked at me expectantly.

I thought hard about what he had said. Although I disliked the outside world, the physical world with all its confusing lessons and hateful unfriendly people, I was stuck in it, so I needed to change my attitude and get on with life. Accept the world and learn to live in it. I learned the spiritual world easily, now it was time to balance myself out and learn to live in the two worlds harmoniously. An awfully big task if you ask me. But with a determined frame of mind, I knew I could accomplish it.

I hadn't even realized we had been standing there in complete silence, until Raa broke the silent air by stretching his long, orange body, releasing a mighty feline yawn, and wandered outside. John turned to me with his clear eyes and I noticed the red streaks in his aura had disappeared and in its place was all the blue and gold that normally radiated there.

"Well, you're here," he said quietly. I knew he had listened in on my thoughts and was no longer angry with me. "We might as well make the best out of the time and teach you something."

I smiled my reply.

"Let's see, what do we have here?" John asked as he pointed to the corner that Raa had just vacated. There stood a beautiful mirror in a gold carved frame.

"Where did that come from?" I asked, all excited. The questions just kept tumbling out of me. "Is it magic? What are we going to do with the mirror, John? Oh, it's so beautiful! I've never seen anything quite so nice."

"When you calm down, we'll see what you can learn

about yourself by looking into your own image," John said, interrupting my eager questioning. I made a zipping motion across my lips, indicating I was quieting down so we could start the lesson.

"Now Carol, I want you to sit in front of the mirror and look into your eyes," John began.

I settled myself directly in front of the mirror, in front of my image, and looked. Disappointed, I saw only my eyes. Although they were nice, brown, round eyes. But what did he wish for me to see?

"Look into the dark parts of your eyes. Do you see something inside there?" John asked, gently urging me to go deeper.

I looked right into the dark parts as he instructed and I saw me, my body, my face looking back at me. I felt John's reassuring pat on the shoulder as if to silently say, "Okay, you're on the right track."

"Now look at you inside of your eye. Are both images the same?" he asked.

Upon instruction, I looked deeper and closer at the picture of myself in my eye. "No," I said firmly, "the one on the right side is fainter than the one on the left. The left one is much stronger. Why is that?"

"Well, it's because the left side of you, which is your intuition and spiritual side, is confident and highly developed while the right side, which is your physical world, is very weak and under developed because of your insecurities about school and the physical world in general. What I mean to say, is you're not in balance." John became thoughtful as he continued on in his explanation, "That's what your teachers in school are trying to tell you and you don't want to listen to them." Suddenly, he became somewhat stern, "I want you to do your homework and try, really try, in school to do your absolute best and everyday look in a mirror and see if that right image becomes as strong as your left one. It's important for both images to be strong and confident."

I have to balance living in two worlds, I thought to myself, summing up his lecture.

The cave began to grow dark, the shadows from the late afternoon sun blended into darkness. The only light source came from the fire, smoldering against the cold night air. I decided it was late, too late to try to walk home, so spending the night was my only answer.

I welcomed the aloneness from my family's prying questions, and settled once again in front of the wondrous mirror to do a little more looking. Now that it had grown dark in the cave, the image reflected back at me somehow was changed. I was no longer looking at Carol, yet I was. My features seemed to meld in and out to form other faces. First, a man's face appeared and I could barely make out a soldier's hat and blue eyes. My eyes are brown, I realized with a start. Then the image wavered and changed, and I saw a heavyset black woman in its place. I noticed her eyes were filled with pain and they stared, unblinking, back at me. "John," I called cautiously, not really afraid, but more puzzled, unsure. "Who are these people I see looking back at me?"

John appeared beside me and said quietly, "That's you, Carol. See that black woman? That is you in another lifetime. Tell me about her. Look into her face and tell me what you see."

I looked directly into those pained eyes and spoke from what I saw. "She's had a lot of pain. I think maybe she was a slave? She feels all alone. Her spiritual energy is real high and I think she is still alive because of her faith. Her faith gives her hope." It felt strange, I was talking without really thinking first. The words seemed to flow from my eyes out my mouth, not stopping to process first in my brain. Yet everything I said, I really believed was true.

"That's how you felt in that life," John said, reading my thoughts.

Once again the image wavered and shifted to meld into

another face. This time it was the face of a very stern woman. Her eyes were small and hardened with meanness. The cold in them sliced right through me without so much as a flinch from her. "John, this person is so mean," I said again without thinking, "Is that me, too?"

"Yes, you've had many lifetimes, Carol. What can you tell me about this one?"

"Well, she's been hurt, both often and deeply. And she doesn't trust anyone, so she never lets anyone get close to her. That stern look she carries is to keep people away. She's very strong, with a lot of yellow around her. She's really smart, too." I no sooner said this when she faded out and the image returned to my own once again. "This is so fun!" I said, and before I knew it, another barrage of questions came tumbling out. "Is this a magic mirror? How does it work? What—"

"If you want to learn more," John interrupted me head on, "you need to be in that calm state, so settle down and I'll give you a few answers to your questions." He then took a stick that had been lying close by and drew a circle in the dirt next to the fire. "Look at the circle and tell me what you see."

I did as he said and looked at the circle intensely. "Well, it's round," I said finally.

"Carol, look at the circle. It has no beginning or end, it's constant, just like life," John said. "Let's say this circle represents all life and all knowledge, and is full and complete with no true beginning or end."

Just then, the firelight flickered, causing the shadowed shape to change dimensions, yet even with the fluctuation of light it remained whole, complete, without an ending or beginning.

"Look at how the circle is ever moving and changing. It's always shifting to maintain its perfect wholeness. Now I want you to draw another circle inside this large one." John made a motion for me to begin.

I used my index finger to draw a small circle inside

John's larger one.

"Now, let me ask you this question: Does your circle take away from the larger circle?" he asked.

I thought for a moment. Then a flash filled my head and I quickly answered, "It doesn't take away from the larger circle, it's just inside of and a part of the larger one."

"Alright," John said and I could tell I was on the right track. "That smaller circle represents you now, in the present, and you don't take away from, but you can experience knowledge from, the larger orb.

"All life is going on right now. People measure life by time so they can have some order to it. But in the spirit world there is no time or space. When you take your fences off of yourself as you know you to be in this world, then you can get a glimpse of all of you, that includes these other people we call past lives or future lives. They are really lives that are going on right now." John finished his explanation and moved into another instruction, "Carol, you can do this at home. Just light a candle at night so there is very little light present and sit in front of your mirror. Relax your mind and the other parts of you will appear, just like it has here."

I turned back to the mirror and looked deep into myself, trying to remain calm and relaxed. Sure enough, another face came looking back at me, this time it was an Oriental man with a big smile and a twinkle in his merry eyes. It made me feel happy, bubbly, with a kind of mischievous energy.

John's voice emerged from the background, "Tell me what you get from this person, Carol."

"He likes to have fun," I said, again without thinking. "He's a real happy person. He likes kids, too, I can tell by the way his eyes sparkle. He's also a storyteller, I think. He likes to teach kids through stories."

"You're right," John said encouragingly. "You have inside you everything these people have learned, as well as many more people from your other lives. That knowledge is all yours and all you have to do is pull from this knowledge what you need. It will help you with your schooling and you can surprise your teacher with how smart you really are."

That made me really excited, imagining how surprised my teachers would be when I showed them I could learn. I got up to throw another log on the disintegrating fire, knowing the warmth would be needed to get me through the chilly night. When I turned back around the beautiful mirror had just disappeared.

"Where did it go?" I cried. "I wasn't through with it yet!"

"Yes, you are," John soothed. "You've had enough for one day, now it's time to rest your mind as well as your body. There's a lot of learning that goes on when you sit and contemplate what you have experienced. So, now I want you to lie down and rest, think about who you really are . . ." His voice drifted off as I lay down on my crudely made bed of pine needles and an old sheet, falling fast asleep as my head hit the pine needle pillow.

Morning arrived, and I was greeted with its freezing salutation and a stiff body. The fire had died sometime during the night and the coals were barely smoking, quickly extinguishing from the cold morning air. I jumped up and quickly threw some pine cones and wood on the dwindling fire to get it started again. Soon it was alive with flames, licking the air with its heat and light.

As I began to fully awaken, standing by the fire warming my front, I realized John and Raa were no where to be found. I turned around to warm my back and as I did so, the memory of the night before filled my brain as fresh and vibrant as if I had just experienced it. It made me wonder some more about past and future lives, and about how I could use the knowledge from my other lives to learn in school. The remainder of the morning was spent in "digestion", as John referred to the mulling over and acceptance of thoughts.

It was late in the afternoon before John and Raa

materialized in the cave. John carried with him a glass filled with a slightly steaming honey-colored substance.

"Had enough time?" he asked with a warm, reassuring smile. He handed me the glass and indicated I should drink it.

I reached for the golden substance, and as I drank it down, I felt the sweet liquid warm me from the inside out.

"I have a question," I pondered, enjoying the remains of the golden liquid sliding down my throat and dripping into my stomach. "How do I get the information from my other lives?"

"Well, it's like this," John mused. "When the teacher is talking, listen to what he is saying, but also listen with your inner ear and your inner eye. Then the information will come to you. Trust that knowledge that you receive and you will have much better marks in school."

I looked at him with such confusion, he felt compelled to explain further.

"Okay, let's say I'm your teacher," he started in his gentle tone, "and I want to know what 21 plus 36 equals. Listen and look for the answer. What did you come up with inside your head when I asked you that, Carol?"

Without hesitation I replied, "57?"

"Right!" John shouted. "See? You can add and do math, you just need to know what works best for you, so you can get the correct answers. When you let the picture inside your mind's eye come forth, you always will have the right answer. Now, regretfully, it's time for you to return home. I'm sure your mother must be worried about you."

"Worried doesn't even cover it. John, she is going to be awfully angry at me for not going to school yesterday and not coming home last night," I cried. "What should I do?"

"Carol, remember when we were at the pond, when you were working on healing your brother Mark?" I nodded my head, I remembered clearly. It was the same time I had lied next to the water and cleansed my soul. "Well, do you remember what you did to send your love out to your family?"

I thought a moment. "Pink!" I exclaimed.

"Yes," John replied. He was happy I retained my lesson.

"Pink is the color of love and understanding," I repeated, paraphrasing what John had told me that day. "I'll put her in the pink light while I walk home."

John was nodding his head in agreement. "Put her into a good space before you get home and it will work, you'll see . . ." He waved a small good-bye as I started my descent down the mountain.

I had quite a bit of work ahead of me on the walk home, and I didn't hesitate to get started on it. The whole way home I threw balls of pink energy at the house. I visualized the ball of pink light melt over my mother. I used my imagination like I've never used it before, with determination.

As I approached the house, I saw smoke curling up from the chimney and a small knot of fear welled up inside of me. Immediately I told myself to stop the fear, the light and love were working for me. The knot slowly dissolved and I felt strong again as I entered the kitchen, running smack into my mother.

Forgive everybody
for
everything now

The better way of living

few know how

What few can do Today

many can do Tomorrow

absolute forgiveness

the true spiritual Bow

CHAPTER EIGHT

Lifetimes

I closed the door quietly behind me, the image of love streaming from me to my mother close in my mind. She had her back to me, stirring the potatoes quickly in the frying pan so as not to burn them. The final chorus of "You are my Sunshine" filled the kitchen, the tune mingling with the sound of the spatula scraping the pan. As she finished the song, she turned to take the potatoes off the flame and met me head on. Her usual look of worry and work was replaced by a stern look intended only for me. I shrank back a little from the look, but held my ground. The pink light still danced in my inner eye and I held to the image like a drowning man holds to a life preserver.

Finally, she broke the silence. "Well, well, look what the cat drug in," she said in cool and quiet tone. "I see you finally decided to come home. Ricky had to do your chores while you were away. I'll tell you, young lady, he's mad as can be at you, so I'd watch my P's and Q's if I were you. We both know his temper." She said all this in that same cool, even tone.

I felt my stomach drop to the floor when she mentioned Ricky. I was afraid of Ricky almost more than of my mother. The image of his snarling, angry temper filled my mind when I thought of him. I shuddered and kept quiet, saying nothing in my own defense seemed better than speaking right now. And what could I tell her anyway? That I'd been up in the mountains with John and Raa learning all sorts of important things? No, that wouldn't be wise.

"I realize nothing I say or do will stop you from doing exactly what you want to do, so don't expect me to waste my time screaming or yelling at you. I'm not even going to punish you, either. Only, I'm not going to tell Ricky what to do or say either. So you're going to have to take care of yourself where Ricky is concerned," she said, her back turned again as she cleaned vegetables in a bowl of water. "Maybe that's the best punishment I can give you, knowing his temper and all." She seemed to be speaking now more to herself than to me. "I'm not even going to ask you what you have to say for yourself since I'm not up to one of your crazy stories right now. Besides, if a girl like you wants to freeze her behind out there in this kind of weather, far be it for me if I'm going to stop you." She continued her preparations for dinner and ignored me. I knew that the conversation was now closed.

I fell in beside her to help with dinner, relief mixed with worry. I remembered one time when Ricky broke all the windows in his room because he didn't get his way. I shuddered when I remembered the glass shattering and flying as he swung a broomstick in a frenzied tantrum. He would definitely be a challenge for me.

After I finished every morsel on my plate, I hurried to wash up and get to my room, for I heard the boys advancing to the kitchen and I wished to be well out of their sight and teasing.

I changed into my nightgown and slipped under the covers in my favorite position, and began to think about Ricky. The pink light worked on my mother, now I hoped it would work on him.

The sound of the long, snake-like whip crackled and snapped against my skin. At first I felt nothing, a numbing sensation almost. Then the pain. Oh, the pain, it bit and stung to the very core of my being. I looked over my shoulder, a fleeting glance at the man who was responsible for this severe and unbearable pain. I felt the racking pain overtake my body, my consciousness was slipping quickly, but with one eye I saw the man who was beating me. His face was contorted in a gross sort of pleasure, an enjoyment at releasing pain onto someone else. His face suddenly turned into Ricky's face. With another raise of his hand, another expression of pleasure, another crack of that horrible whip, I flinched and jumped at the pain . . . and awoke in a cold sweat.

What a nightmare. I turned over and tried to go back to sleep, but no matter how hard I tried to fall into a dreamless sleep, the nightmare kept reoccuring all night long.

When morning came, I welcomed its early light and coldness like I never had before. Anything to relieve me from that awful dream. Even my chores were a welcomed event, something to take my mind off the images of the night before. Betsy greeted me with her usual round-eyed look of gratitude. Her udder was full and ready to burst, since she disliked Ricky milking her the day before, she had held back almost half of the amount she usually gave forth. She relaxed as I gently began to release her of her milk and I could sense it made her feel new again. I patted her affectionately on the back when the job was over and whispered in her ear that I would never do that to her again. I think she understood me because she turned her head around and looked me straight in the eyes with a look of pure love.

The rest of my chores consisted of feeding the chickens and throwing some hay out for the young calves, wobbling around on new legs, they were the most fun of all. As I left the hay barn I ran face to face into none other than Ricky. The dark look he gave me made my skin crawl, and his aura was muddled with a murky red radiating around his head. I watched his thoughts take form and clearly saw he seeked revenge. He grabbed an old corn cob and slowly hit his palm with it. He didn't say a word, but his face had an evil smirk intact. I turned and ran to the house as fast as my small legs would carry me. Before I reached the screen door, I felt the whoosh of the corn cob as it whizzed by my ear at a deadly speed. That wasn't half as scary as his energy which felt like darts honing in on their target, the target being me.

Once inside the safety of the house, I washed my hands and went to my room. I sat down on the bed and took some deep, slow breaths. They started to calm me down as I concentrated on inhaling deeply, then holding it in, and letting the air escape slowly.

Okay, I thought to myself, if there's no time and space like John said, and I can get knowledge from my other lives, then I can get strength from them as well. I took in another lung full of air, and exhaled slowly, finally ready to get my thoughts in order. The light worked once before, I reminded myself, it will work again. All I have to do is believe and have faith in my power to create my own world.

I asked for help from all my highest, most powerful teachers and guides. As I did so, the image in my mind's eye first focused on John. Then an image of Christ appeared which gave me intense strength and love for this Christ image. Suddenly, a strong feeling started to move inside me, like a warming, healing heat, sort of a cross between hot and cold simultaneously. This tingling heat moved up to my heart area and it sat there for a moment. I knew something extraordinary was happening, so I just let the experience take its own form. Soon the feeling evaporated and in its place was a strong and safe feeling. I opened my eyes and saw many other forms in the room with me. It was as if my room was filled with people all looking at me. It almost over-whelmed me, I asked for their help and here they stood. I looked around, amazed at first, then slowly accepting the experience. Many of them were there, yet they weren't there, more like faint images. I thanked them for coming to help me and this seemed to signify their departure. They disappeared, yet I still felt them with me.

It was now time to study. I picked up one of my school books and settled into a learning mode. I studied for what seemed like hours, until I heard my mother call for me to do my chores.

I threw on my coat and headed toward the stairs. As I passed by my brother's room, I caught the last part of a conversation between Ricky and Peter.

"I'm going to make Carol sweat it out," I heard Ricky say, a bit maliciously, and Peter joined in in a wicked laughter. The moment their laughter drifted out to me, a cold shiver went down my spine. I took the stairs two at a time, rushing to get away from there. I didn't want Ricky to see me, lest he decide to make me "sweat it out".

Fear controlled my movements through all my chores, and I knew Betsy sensed my fear because she jumped when I touched her, her own look of fear mirrored my own. I passed the boys going out to milk their cows. I kept my head down to avoid any eye contact and without incident, made it safely into the house.

Dinner that night was a struggle. I ate as quietly and unobtrusively as possible, yet I still felt at least one pair of eyes on me: Ricky's. I felt his eyes bore into me, willing me to look up. But I avoided his stare and concentrated on eating my beans and potatoes. I knew if I so much as glanced his way, I'd get an eyeful of that evil smirk he was so proud of possessing. I couldn't face him, not yet, not until I worked on him longer.

I wanted to hurry up, finish my dinner and escape to the safety of my room, but tonight it was my turn to do the dishes, so I paced myself with eating, and waited until everyone else, Ricky included, left the kitchen before I began clearing the table and washing dishes. This avoiding thing is working for now, I thought to myself as I scraped a stubborn potato from the frying pan, but I couldn't avoid Ricky for the rest of my life. No, I wanted him to love me, forgive me, and if we couldn't be equals as the boys had so ardently pointed out before, then at least tolerant, maybe even a little like friends. I knew I had to try even harder to work on him, I wanted this nastiness to end.

That night lying in my bed, after I heard my mother's heavy steps take her to bed, I started my work again. I sat up and wrapped my blankets around me in the middle of the bed. I closed my eyes, filled my lungs with the cool, fresh air that only the night time can bring, and asked, once again, for help from all the power in the universe.

The movement, at first, started subtly, growing more and more as the powers came close. Then the heat, ever so faintly, began to buzz in my heart center. Like a lazy bumblebee, it buzzed slowly, around and around, until a steady rhythm took its place and the heat filled my entire body. That's when I visualized Ricky sitting inside my heart surrounded by all this warmth. I asked him to free me.

"Free me, Ricky," I whispered in my mind. "I am so sorry if I hurt you in any way."

I saw him laughing as I spoke to him. Then I heard ever so faintly, yet clearly, "You didn't hurt me. I'm having fun with you," he said.

I felt love growing deeper, deeper in my heart center. Ricky, still sitting inside the center, started to shift and move. I could see all of the love was penetrating him, filling him up.

"I love you, Ricky," I said softly, out loud. It was met with a wink. He winked at me. Then I knew he loved me too, in his own way. I inhaled a few more deep breaths and felt the love swirling inside me. I knew I could sleep now, so I snuggled down in bed, surrounded by love, which gently lulled me to sleep.

The whip cracked mercilessly as it hit my skin. The pain

shot through every part of my body, acute and biting. I thought I wouldn't last through another round of the whip, when I felt someone untie my hands. My body slumped to the ground, devoid of any possible functioning of my limbs. As my face pressed into the dirt, I saw a pair of black boots so close to my head, I could smell their leathery form. I turned only my eyes to look at my master standing over me.

"Well, maybe you've learned your lesson this time, Bitch," he slurred. I looked deep into his eyes. I knew it was Ricky even though they looked nothing alike. It was the hate and power in his eyes that gave him away. As I looked at him, I let the love flow out of my heart toward him, and I thought to myself, "I forgive you. You have no idea what you're doing . . ."

I awoke with a start. It was still dark in my tiny room, but I knew it must be early morning. My dream came rushing back to me, as vibrant and clear as if I was experiencing it again. So, Ricky and I had lived in that lifetime together and he was my master, a cruel and angry one at that. Was that why he was so mean and bitter now? He must be working out his past with me.

I left the bed to light a candle, and I moved over to where the mirror was above the dresser. I tried to relax, take deep breaths, calm myself so I could see if there were any other faces looking back at me. Nothing happened. "John's mirror must be magic," I thought sleepily as I crawled back into bed and fell into an instant slumber.

The next day being Sunday, everyone went their own way doing chores, finishing homework, preparing for the coming week of school.

Late that afternoon I bumped into Ricky. I was coming out the back door when I literally bumped into him leaning against the porch beam. He reached out to steady me, so I wouldn't fall from the impact and stood me upright. His touch was not the usual rough shove, but a softer, gentler, helping touch. I looked up at him, startled by the fact that I had really run into him, and he winked at me in return. He winked, just like he did in my heart center last night. A warmth filled my body and I couldn't stop a small smile from escaping. I had gotten through to him!

The whole way to the barn I felt like jumping and clapping with joy. It worked, it worked! I kept repeating that phrase through the rest of my chores. What a magnificent feeling! But just as a precaution, I decided I would work just a teeny bit more on him tonight, just to make sure.

That night I wrapped blankets around me again, lit the candle, and made my way over to my mirror. As I sat there, I first looked in the mirror at my pupils. Then I noticed my reflection looking back at me.

"Still no change," I sighed as I saw my one side still strong and the other still weak. I continued to stare when I felt something come around my head. There in the mirror was the mean looking woman with the long, protruding nose I had seen before. She stared silently down her nose at me, a disapproving line set her mouth. I felt her hurt and anger, and tried to look even deeper into her. Suddenly, I felt myself floating, lifting up, up and out of my physical body. I felt myself standing next to a wall. Was it my wall? No. I was so close to this wall, I was almost inside it. Then I saw a room, almost a hovel, bare with just a crudely made fireplace, a thin wooden bed, and a simple wood chair. On the bed sat a man in torn clothing. He was whittling on a piece of wood, making a flute. It was too early to tell it was a flute, but I somehow knew that was what he was whittling. I kept my eyes riveted on him. He suddenly stopped whittling, setting the knife and wood on the bed, and turned in my direction. He slowly stood up and walked deliberately toward me. He looked at me with squinting eyes, as if he was straining to barely see me in the wall. Were those eyes looking out, he seemed to say with his expression, or a pattern in the old wood wall? He was about a foot away from me when our eyes met and locked. An electric bolt shot through me, penetrating every cell in my soul body, knocking me back with a jolt, back into my room and my physical body with a loud thud.

I just sat there, blinking, in stunned silence. What just happened here? I was a little panicky until I heard John's voice, soothing, in my inner ear.

"Well, Carol, you just met another part of yourself," he said. "When the two of you made contact, your energies shot electricity through the both of you." Then he chuckled quietly at his next words, "Can you imagine how he's feeling right now, after seeing you in his wall and then getting blitz with an electric shock on top of all that? That other part of you probably doesn't even know what hit him!" John began to all out laugh, which made me laugh, too, although part of my laughter was a laughter of relief.

"By working with Ricky," John began, after his laughing jag had calmed down, "using your heart center to help him to feel love, you also are helping him to become more understanding to the woman you see as a black slave. That past will also change as this one will when Ricky starts to change. When one lifetime makes a major change, it starts a chain reaction and things start changing in all lifetimes."

"Why did I see that angry and mean woman, John? And right after that, I experienced leaving my body, standing in the wall, and looking at that other part of me? Why—"

John interrupted my incessant questioning. "So many questions!" he laughed. Then in all seriousness, he looked deep into my eyes. It felt like he was looking into my soul. Very calmly he said, "Remember when your mother tricked you into telling her what you were doing with the spirits in this house?" I nodded my head. I remembered all too clearly the hurt and betrayal it brought upon me. "This woman you see is another part of you from another life who had felt the same pain. That's why she looks as though she doesn't trust anyone. You, my dear, still have some of that pain inside you from your family. The part of you that you call 'the mean-looking woman' ties into that fear and pain. Every time you have that experience it's because there's a deeper part of you that's afraid your mother will hurt you again as badly as she did in the past.

"Carol, I've helped to block her from seeing you work with the souls trapped here. And you keep the doors locked when you're in your own room. And, we have the safety of the mountains to go to where we can learn, so she won't hurt you, at least, not now.

"When you think of your family, especially your mother, send love and forgiveness for they don't realize what they're doing."

That is so hard to do, I thought to myself.

"It might be hard to do," John said out loud, clearly eavesdropping on my thoughts, "but it always works, doesn't it?" He smiled widely. "Besides, the love and forgiveness isn't so much for them as it is for you. When you let go of the pain inside you, you will feel clear. That will also help you to clear out the hurt for that woman who keeps coming up from other lifetimes. What you do in this life helps clear and clean other lives as well. Just like the way it helped the black woman inside you and your brother Ricky."

It all started to make sense now, like a puzzle coming together to form an intricate picture from all its individual pieces.

"Carol, think back, remember when you had dreams of war. You were a soldier and deeply afraid of death. Well, that lifetime as Carl the soldier helped you to understand your father's death, just like the slave helped you to let go of anger and pain with Ricky. Now that part of you that's hurt and angry with your mother needs understanding and clearing." He paused to let it all sink in. The puzzle became more complete with each word he said. "You have a lot of work to do in this lifetime, Carol, and it's going to take time and forgiveness and a lot of understanding . . ."

I crawled under the covers while John helped me to pull them up over my chin. My head was spinning with so much thought. I started thinking about this thing called life. How it's a constant circle of lifetimes, moving and changing with no beginning or end, yet all inter-aligned with each other. I thought about how I can help another life or part of myself through clearing and cleaning with love and forgiveness. My head spinning with ideas, I turned to say good night to John, but he had disappeared. I sighed a little sigh for all that I learned and all the more that I have to learn.

"Goodnight, John," I whispered into the night, "wherever you are . . ."

TAPES BY CAROL LOVEJOY

These creative visualization tapes have been utilized by many of Carol's clients with extraordinary results. Now Carol makes these tapes available to you to use and enjoy. To order any of the 34 tapes described below, just complete the order form directly following this list of tapes.

Side I of each tape is a visualization and relaxation technique, while side II provides positive affirmations to compliment the meditations of side I.

#1 BALANCING ENERGY CENTERS
This tape takes you into a place of deep relaxation where you are guided through a visualization exercise, aligning and balancing your seven major energy centers.

#2 SPIRIT GUIDES
Who are your spirit guides? This visualization exercise will introduce you to your own guides so you can know, feel, see, communicate, and learn from them.

#3 GOALS — UNIVERSAL HEARTBEAT
Establish your wealth today by releasing blocks and aligning your goals with the universal power and accepting your manifestation of good in your life NOW.

#4 YOUR HUB FOR DRAWING IN CLIENTELE AND WEALTH
This meditation will establish your hub and open doors that draw in clientele for a prosperous business.

#5 BALANCING THE MALE AND FEMALE
Learn how to communicate with these two parts of yourself by learning what you can do to help your female and male beings balance and flow harmoniously. The results are learning about self-loving-self and experiencing balance in all parts of life.

#6 HIGHER SELF
See different things to help you understand your own personality make-up. Meet your own higher self, communicate, and receive answers for and about yourself.

#7 LETTING GO WITH LOVE AND FORGIVENESS
Holding on to hurt feelings, anger, resentment and things of the past will hold you back and waste your energy. This can add negative power to the person or situation. In this process you can let go of the negative to feel love and experience forgiveness by releasing the person or situation all together.

#8 SELF-HEALING

Love heals when you allow the love energy of your higher self to flow through your hands into your body, healing and loving every part of your spirit mind and body.

#9 WEIGHT LOSS

This technique is designed to allow you to let go of physical and emotional blocks within you which cause you to keep on unwanted weight. Plus, learn how to love yourself and reshape your body to the perfect shape and size, allowing the new you to manifest.

#10 YOUR ANIMAL GUIDE

See and get to know your animal guide. Ask questions about yourself, your past and your present as well as learn how to call on your animal guide for future guidance and protection.

#11 SPIRITUAL GOALS

Have you ever wondered, why you are here? What are you doing on this earth plane? This tape will help you to learn more about your own spiritual identity.

#12 YOUR AURA

See your own energy field, or colors, vibrating for you. Learn what the colors are and what they mean.

#13 CRYSTAL PYRAMID

This meditation will clean you energy field and establish a protection barrier around you by using the shape of the pyramid.

#14 HOUSE CLEANING

Mental house cleaning will clean out all the negative energy and replace it with positive energy, surrounding you with harmonious, peaceful, energy in your home, office, social gatherings, etc.

#15 PAST LIVES

See and know your past lives to better understand who you are now, in your present life. This is an informative and fun way to learn about yourself.

#16 BLOCKS FROM PAST LIVES

Learn to release blocks from your past lives so that you can experience success easily, smoothly, and perfectly in this life.

#17 PEOPLE AND PAST LIVES

In this creative process you look at people from now and how they relate to your past life so you can better understand your relationships with others. Also, you will release negative experiences so you can have a positive relationship now.

#18 SUBJECTIVE COMMUNICATION

Do you have someone in your life whom you would like to help make positive changes in their life? This technique allows you to connect with their higher self so you can communicate and establish a positive and harmonious relationship with that part of themselves and help their higher self to align their physical, mental, and emotional life with their highest good.

#19 PERFECT MATE
This tape will help you to let go of the past, your fears, and anxieties, and replace them with love for self so you are confident and feel worthy to experience the perfect mate in your life.

#20 UNPLUGGING ENERGY CENTERS
This process will help you to clean out the clogged energy of people and situations in your life and will also teach you who and what seems to plug into you.

#21 KNOWING AND LOVING THE CHILD WITHIN
Get to know your own inner-child and lovingly embrace that child within you. By learning to love and accept your own inner-self, it will help you to love and accept a better life for yourself.

#22 HAVING FUN AND RELEASING THE CHILD WITHIN
This creative process will help you to have fun with that child inside of you so you can let go and experience the same carefree fun in your life today more easily, guilt-free, and fear-free.

#23 BREAKING THE WORRY PATTERN
This creative process will help you to clean out the dark, negative worry pattern and set into active motion a positive vibration, so you will experience a positive high in every part of your life.

#24 COMPLETING PROJECTS
Learning to see and experience your project being completed will give you intuitive insight into the project and will fill you with the knowledge, confidence, and energy to move you into that place of completion.

#25 DREAM PROGRAMMING
Use of this visualization process will fine tune you so that you have dream recall and will call forth the subject you desire to dream about. This will give you a wealth of knowledge about yourself, others, and the world.

#26 RELEASING THE DECEASED
Through this process you can help someone who has died to move on over to the other side and let go of the physical world.

#27 SEEING FUTURE EVENTS
This process will allow you to become focused on your inner computer which has all the knowledge. At this time you will ask for information from your computer and view your answers on the screen of your mind, seeing future events for yourself and others.

#28 LONG DISTANCE HEALING
Through complete relaxation you can connect with a person in need of healing. You will visualize this person as balanced and whole in spirit, mind, and body which will align them with their highest healing energy.

#29 HIGHER POWER FOR HELPING SOMEONE MAKE TRANSITIONS
This is a wonderful visualization to help someone take that step from this life to the next plane.

#30 STRESS RELEASE
This process will release stress from all areas of your life keeping you well balanced.

#31 THE UNSPOKEN WORDS
This process will help you to say those unspoken words to the people who have left your life abruptly or have died, so you can complete the relationship and re-establish a process of communication with them in a positive matter. This will help you all to grow and heal.

#32 VIEWING AND RELEASING THE PAST
This visualization will help you to release those feelings of guilt, anger, hurt, or fear and allow you to feel confident, happy, and healthy about yourself and your past.

#33 LOVING RELATIONSHIPS
With the use of this tape, you will work on your relationship on a higher level helping you to establish loving relationships into your life.

#34 WEALTH — A WAY OF LIFE
You can learn to reshape your life into a wealthy, fun, and exciting adventure. Learn the power of beliefs and attitudes, words, secrets, visualization, etc., to bring about the wealth you deserve.*

* This set of four tapes may be purchased for $40.00 and tapes within the set may not be sold separately.

ORDER FORM

If you would like to order **tapes, additional books,** or **be placed on Carol Lovejoy's mailing list,** please fill in the correct information below:

(Print) **Name:** _____

Address: _____

City, State, Zip _____

Telephone: (_____) _____

☐ **YES, I would like to order** _____ **additional *Living in Two Worlds* soft cover book(s) at the cost of $12.95 per book.**

☐ **Please place me on Carol Lovejoy's mailing list.**

Tapes are $10 each or Buy 3 and get 1 FREE!*

Tape #	Quantity	Title	Price ea.	Total

Please make checks or money order payable to:
GOLDEN GLOBE PUBLISHING
P.O. Box 577049
Modesto, CA 95357

Shipping ($1.00 per tape): _____

Shipping (per book): _____

Tax (CA residents only): _____

Total: _____

*Retails stores excluded